Silver State Superlatives

Paul Sebesta

Sebesta Publishing supports the copyrights of human authors. Thank you for reading an authorized edition of this book and for complying with the copyright laws by not reproducing, scanning, or distributing any part of it in any form without written permission from the author. You are supporting writers. For more copyright information, please write to defininglight395@gmail.com

eBook ISBN: 979-8-9905383-6-8

Paperback ISBN: 979-8-9905383-7-5

Cover design by GetCovers.

All artwork and photos © Paul Sebesta, unless otherwise stated

Copyright © 2024 by S. Paul Sebesta

All rights reserved. v.1

Contents

Nevada — 1

Ready, Set, Go! — 9

1. OLDEST — 13
    World's Oldest Living Thing
    Oldest Human Remains Found in North America
    Oldest Rock Art Site in North America
    Oldest Community
    Oldest Building
    Oldest Hotel
    Oldest Saloon
    Oldest Courthouse
    Oldest Gaming License
    Oldest Brothel

2. HIGHEST & LOWEST — 35
    Highest Point
    Highest Paved Road
    Highest Mountain Range

World's Highest Concrete Arch Bridge

Highest Mountain Pass

Highest Historical Site

Highest Lake

Highest & Lowest Recorded Temperatures

Lowest Point

3. LONGEST & SHORTEST — 53

Shortest Highway

Longest Road

Longest-Running Show

Longest Lived Mining Camp

Longest Urban Street

Longest Continuous Unpaved Road

Longest Cathedral-Arch Bridge in the World

Longest Mountain Range

Longest Valley

Longest Stretch of Road Without Services

Longest River

4. LARGEST & SMALLEST — 73

Largest Payout

Largest Alpine Lake in the World

Largest Lakebed in North America

Largest Wildlife Refuge in the Continental U.S.

Largest Hotel-Casino

Largest Body of Water

Largest Hot Spring

Largest State Park

Largest Silver Strike in U.S. History

Smallest Border Town

Smallest State Park

Smallest Community

5. EPIC & AWESOME ... 99

Most Expensive Hotel Room in the World

Most Expensive Cocktail

Most Expensive Restaurant

The Paiute Princess

Deadliest Mining Camp

Tallest Structure

Tallest Waterfall

Nevada's Only Micronation

The Geographical Center of Nevada

Nevada's Only Port City

Most Common Plant

Most Common Tree

Steepest Grade

Rarest Fish in the World

The Most Remote Town with Services

A Couple More Teasers

The Most Isolated Spot in Nevada

Resources ... 155

Acknowledgements ... 161

Acknowledgments

This book is dedicated to the crazy, die-hard Nevadans and their passionate Nevada swan songs.

Nevada
A State of Mind

DON'T LOOK TOO HARD. You won't find this place on any map. In this state, the clanking of the slots or the neon frenzy of the Strip don't apply. Most people perceive Nevada as little more than quick gaming stays, cabarets, cheap buffets, and hearsay. Truth. We're also a state easily and unfairly judged, and not fully understood as many people assume there isn't anything worthwhile outside of either of the Silver State's two metropolitan areas.

Here's some more truth. While anybody can live in Nevada, not everybody will consider themselves a *true* Nevadan.

A Nevada State of Mind begins with a rare outlook to appreciate the simpler things and an ability to marvel at the inner beauty found within, before finally transcending beyond the blazing lights and the rumble of an interstate. Only then by achieving this sense of heart and home, you're left with a lasting and unexpected take on this wonderfully, complex state. This, my friends, is the Nevada State of Mind.

A Labor of Love: The Nine-Year Itch

Slick canyon roads. Long open pavement. This journey began years ago on the most boring day of the week: a Tuesday. It's only fitting that my first historic marker was number 7, a rather uneventful marker at the busiest crossroads in Dayton. I couldn't help but look a bit overly touristy with the huge camera strapped around my neck as commuters drove right by. That's when the notion hit me like a sack of flour.

> *How many people were aware of their state's history in this mad rush?*

> *How many people TRULY held great pride to where they lived?*

> *How many even cared?*

I didn't know the answer, but it struck me that I *did* care.

Deeply.

I cataloged three more markers that day on my way home. A completionist at heart, I vowed to finish Lyon County the following day. True to my word, I bagged Lyon's last remaining marker, number 255... five days later.

In celebration of this conquest, I broke open a cold Dr. Pepper and threw a solo tailgate party, complete with horribly off-key singing in the middle of Wilson Canyon. With nothing but the song of the river humming through the canyon's ramparts, accompanied by a perfect Silver State sunset, the idea for <u>Nevada Landmarks</u> had been born.

When I returned to reality the next day, I figured why not do "one more." It wasn't until halfway through my third county that my quest had morphed into a new all-encompassing mission: to personally record and conquer every Nevada State Historical Marker.

I didn't think about risk, cost, or sanity. Nevada was my home, and I had to go for broke. Boom or Bust. Why not go all in and let it all roll on the green felt, or in this case, the pale green waves of the sagebrush ocean?

> *New friends met along the way: 186*
> *Number of sick days taken: 84*
> *Number of nights beneath the stars: 1,840*
> *Miles driven: 80,000+*
> *Pairs of tires replaced: 4*
> *Nevada Atlases lost: 7*
> *Hours building website: Countless*
> *Gallons of caffeine consumed: Not nearly enough.*

With so much material at my disposal, I taught myself code and strapped on some obsessive research practices to bring attention to the often-forgotten side of the Silver State. I had originally planned the website to be nothing more than a gray database to store my notes (er, chicken scratch) and information I had compiled on site and from behind the wheel, but I was unaware of just how many of my fellow Nevadans shared the same wanderlust.

A generous portion of my marker hunting amounted to endless hours of research in libraries, state archives, and government offices. I filled many weekday break times with working lunches and tedious phone calls. I worked hard labor for ranchers to gain land access and networked with government officials to further the hunt.

All of this hard work made the limelight when *Nevada Landmarks* made its first front-cover newspaper debut and a two-page article in the *Nevada Appeal,* January 18, 2011. A few days later, KOLO 8 News Reno ran a segment on my adventure to capture history.

Day 397: US 6 halfway between Ely and Tonopah, 2010.

We all swoon over a love story, and this journey is a labor of love. I turned down plenty of comfortable beds, warm meals, and clean shaves solely in favor of the quest. I was early to rise and late to rest. I spent half of my nights under the stars imagining life as that of an early Nevadan.

Some call this labor of love a hobby, others liken it to insanity. For me the former doesn't come close to the intense journey, and the latter sounds disturbingly close to reality.

In my quest of tracking every Nevada Historical Marker, a natural love and fascination for Nevada rooted in my veins. Over the course of a decade, the smallest facts and seemingly nonsensical truths about the state suddenly seemed larger than life for your favorite factoid nut.

Silver State Superlatives

A superlative is the utmost degree of something: The Best of the Best in a specific category. And well, this book is a celebration of Nevada's most fascinating superlatives, and some of the coolest quirks that make up our state.

We pride ourselves on having the driest, oldest, biggest, richest, weirdest things we can imagine in a state that's already larger than life. Simply, nothing is normal in Nevada!

Everything contained on the following pages is a result of my exhaustive fascination, research, obsession, whatever-you-wanna-call-it. I've even gone as far as double (and sometimes triple) checking every bit of weirdness in this book to bring you something informative, riveting, and fun.

I invite you to open yourself to the Nevada State of Mind. Whether you're a long-time Nevadan, new transplant, or just a curious truth-seeker, this is a book that will change your perspective of the most interesting state in the Union.

Well then. There's a superlative right there.

Sailing the Sagebrush Sea on Day 293, halfway between Hawthorne and Tonopah on the Gabbs Valley Highway

Searching for Nevada's Landmarks in all seasons. Winter approaches on the edge of Carson Valley, 2019

Vittles & Gas, anyone? The still-beating heart of Ione is like a burst of inspiration in the middle of nowhere.

This old cabin in northeastern Nevada served as an emergency rain shelter in 2019.

Ready, Set, Go!

How Many of These Did You Know?

Before we dig into the main course, let's dive into a few fun-fact appetizers to wet your whistle.

Number One, Baby!

Nevada is the most mountainous state in the country with over 315 mountain ranges. Oh, and these are just the ones that were given names.

Not Just A Desert

Check out a map or any Google view, and you'll lose count of the remaining unnamed ranges scattered statewide! Your busy eyes will find approximately 43 peaks exceeding 10,000 feet in elevation. Quite a surprise for anybody who thinks our state is just a desert!

Battle Born Peeps, Please Stand Up!

At a ratio of 1 to 5, Nevada has the lowest percentage of native-born residents of any state. That means for every five people you have a drink with in Nevada, only one person will have been born here.

Nevada: The Natural State

Oh, that sweet Mama Nature. Nevada has over 44,000 acres of man-made reservoirs, 2,760 miles of streams, 73 designated wilderness areas and 8.6 *million* acres of national forest.

Let 'Em Run

As of 2021, Nevada is home to 75% of the nation's wild horse and burro population.

Watery Wonderland

Despite its arid exterior, approximately 671 year-round streams course through the state of Nevada.

Vice City

Before Reno was "Reno," it was known as "The Cure" after Nevada became the only state that granted legal divorce in 1931. The Virginia Street Bridge would later become known as "Wedding Band Bridge" because new divorcees would walk directly across the street from the courthouse to toss their rings into the Truckee River.

A Whole Lotta Slotta

In 2018, Nevada had 264,100 slot machines. So, just in case you're wondering: *that's one machine for every eleven residents.*

Go, Battle Born!

While the other states were in an uproar, Nevada was the first state to ratify the 15th Amendment: an act that allowed all people the right to vote regardless of race, color, gender, or servitude.

No Time to Waste!

The longest Morse-code telegram ever sent in U.S. History was the Nevada State Constitution—sent in 1864 from Carson City to Washington D.C. Pressed for time and in a hurry for statehood, the state's entire constitution (with grammatical errors included) was sent in a record 92 minutes.

Precious in Metals

Nevada is the largest gold and silver producer in the nation, and 4th largest gold producer in the world behind China, Australia, and Russia. An estimated $400+ billion in gold and silver has been mined over Nevada's 164-year lifespan.

There. How'd that taste? We're just getting started!

OLDEST

Nevada is renowned for her wisdom and resiliency, so to be crowned the title of "Nevada's Oldest" might be the mightiest honor in the state.

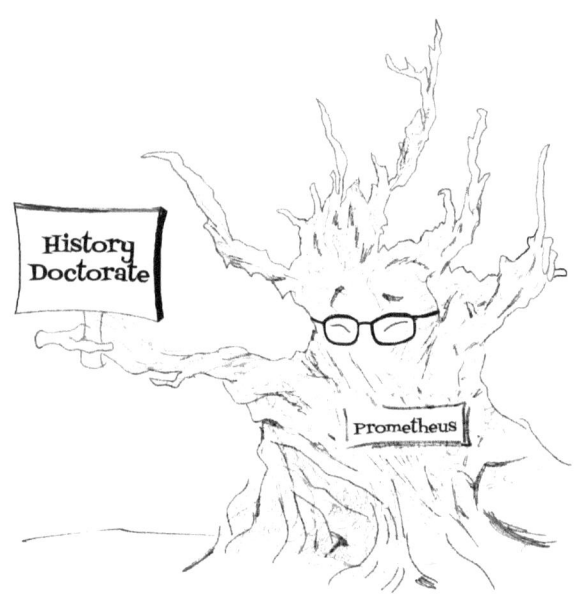

World's Oldest Living Thing

The Bristlecone Pine *(Pinus longeava)* is a form of life without rival or competition. Those lucky enough to stand in the presence of a beguiling Bristlecone will instantly know that these players in the game of life are downright senseis. These are tenured souls that find their home at the top of about two dozen mountain ranges in the Great Basin.

These remarkable beauties make their home in the arctic cold tundra above 11,000 feet. Like ragged old renegades, they grow best when conditions are the most extreme often among rocky, wind facing slopes and snow battered basins inhabited by few other forms of life.

To the Bristlecone, the more challenging, the more XP.

Forests of Bristlecones mainly consist of about twelve to fourteen sizeable and grotesque trees with a beauty that only Nevadans will easily appreciate. In particular, the White and Snake Ranges are home to not only the best known and greatest concentration of these trees, but also the oldest Bristlecones found in the world.

Additionally Bristlecones just don't die easily. One tree alone can cling to life by a single strand of bark or even a mere string of residual resin. Others take on a more tantalizing display of gnarled trunks and naked limbs. It's only fitting that this "never-say-die" overachiever proudly represents Nevada as our state tree.

Fallen Prometheus

In 1964, Donald Currey, a young geology doctoral student from the University of North Carolina, was given permission to study Bristlecone Pines thriving in a grove at the base of Wheeler Peak. He and his team began studying tree rings to determine their exact age and the U.S. Forest Service ultimately granted him special permission to take core samples from any specific tree that piqued his interest.

However, there was a problem. Locating a specific core sample was an arduous task due to the tree's trademark gnarling. For correctly dating the tree, and rather than deal with the headache brought on by sampling, Currey opted instead to completely remove his chosen tree.

Then he found it: a wonderfully monstrous oddity that later became known as "Prometheus," a huge tree that looked to be one of the largest in the grove. Upon locating Ol' Prom, the

Forest Service expressed concern, but eventually gave Currey the authority to chop it down.

In just a few heartbeats, Prometheus was felled by a chainsaw. The researchers lost count after the astounding total number of 5,700 rings. With each ring marking approximately one year of growth, Prometheus revealed its godly status as the WORLD'S OLDEST LIVING THING before his tragic demise.

The Timeline of an Ancient Bristlecone

3200 BP: Prometheus was a young adolescent, when the first cities, and civilization as we know it, were built by the Sumerians in the Indus Valley.

1274 BP: Ramses the II, also known as Ramses the Great, began his reign as the third king in Egypt when Prometheus approached his prime.

30 BP: Prometheus had reached the middle of his life upon the death of Cleopatra, the last Pharoah of the ancient Egyptian Empire.

1100 AD: Prometheus was almost approaching retirement age while Europeans began sailing west to explore the New World.

1620 AD: Prometheus had been living a life of leisure for a few centuries as colonists settled Jamestown, Virginia.

1870 AD: Prometheus witnessed the entirety of the Old West from atop his perch at 11,500 feet!

Oldest Human Remains Found in North America

In 1940, the husband and wife archaeological team of Sydney and Georgia Wheeler found the remains of several people wrapped in reed matting, resting in a shallow grave in a rock shelter just outside of Fallon. With the assistance of the locals, the Wheelers recovered 67 artifacts from the cave.

The Nevada State Museum initially estimated the items to be between an astounding 1,500 and 2,000 years old.

But one set of remains was found buried much deeper than the others, partially mummified from the head to the right shoulder. Their mystery man was a significant find, but it would take two years to unravel the depth of his antiquity. Scientists at the University of California, Riverside dated his hair samples to about 10,600 years! Their "Spirit Cave Man" became THE OLDEST KNOWN MUMMY ON THE CONTINENT.

Studying the Mystery Man

After the discovery, scientists went deep into finding the historical depths of their mystery mummy. They built models of his head, reconstructed his facial features in clay, and analyzed the materials found with the burial site, including his dried excrement to unravel his lifestyle. It was at this time they determined that he and his clan lived in a marsh at the edges of the receding Lake Lahontan where his people caught fish, harvested lush plants, and utilized stone points to hunt game.

The team determined that he was about 45 years old when he died, a ripe old age for the time.

Possibly hours after his death, he was wrapped in a blanket of rabbit fur and laid upon a mat of native hemp fibers. His people then placed his feet in moccasins with leather soles and marmot hide tops.

Spirit Cave Man had two partially healed skull fractures as though he had been hit with a blunt object. Shortly before he died, his teeth became infected, which probably led to blood poisoning. His people cared for him to the end, as evidenced by the ground up fish remains still in his stomach, but he died shortly after that meal.

Clan members carried his body to the shallow cave, dug a grave, and placed him inside the rock shelter, later known as Spirit Cave where he was laid on his right side with his hand resting beneath his chin.

Naturally, the discovery of Spirit Cave Man generated quite the publicity by besting another ancient set of remains: Kennewick Man, dated at over 9,000 years old, who at the time was the oldest set of remains in North America.

 THE SITE OF SPIRIT CAVE MAN'S DISCOVERY CAN BE SEEN BY GUIDED TOUR ONLY.

Even though you can easily reach the site by car, the cave's entrance has been gated off to keep out vandals. At nearby Grimes Point, you can take a cool hour's stroll through some of the state's most accessible rock art — all of which have a direct correlation to Spirit Cave Man. For your tour of Hidden Cave, call the Churchill County Museum at *(775) 423-3677*.

Oldest Rock Art Site in North America

Our state is inundated with some of the most extensive petroglyphs in the world—ancient rock art made by ancient peoples—due in great part to Nevada's varying topography and extensive geologic time scale.

Researchers estimate over 1,100 rock art sites exist in Nevada alone—most of which are found along ancient lake beds and valley floors.

Around 1960, researchers from the University of Nevada discovered a shoreline rife with petroglyphs along Winnemucca Lake. This fascinating location had managed to stay off the grid during other booms of discovery, most likely because of the lake's geographic isolation, seasonal shoreline, and hazardous mud flats—leaving the petroglyphs mostly inaccessible in the colder months.

A recent analysis suggests that these petroglyphs date between 10,500 and 14,800 years ago, making them THE OLDEST ROCK ART EVER FOUND IN NORTH AMERICA.

Ancestry in Abstract

On a patch of western shoreline sit several limestone boulders with deep, ancient carvings; some resemble vegetation, such as trees and leaves, whereas other more abstract designs look like ovals or diamonds in a chain. Although Winnemucca Lake is barren today, in days gone by, the ancient sea was so full of water it would have submerged the petroglyphs, thus naturally preserving them for generations.

After thorough carbon dating, University of Colorado paleoclimatologist Larry Benson revealed that the carbonate film under the petroglyphs dated back roughly 14,800 years!

Later, he dated an additional layer of carbonate that had coated the rock art to about 10,500 years ago. This concludes that the art was crafted somewhere between these two points in time.

> THE WINNEMUCCA LAKE PETROGLYPHS HAVE BEEN SCIENTIFICALLY CATALOGED AS *PETROGLYPH SITE WDL12*.
> The site is located 25 miles north of Nixon off of SR 447 within the Pyramid lake Reservation. In the effort to preserve them, there is no direct road, trail, or sign pointing to the petroglyphs. Please adhere to the strict *"No Trespassing"* signs along the highway as the site is federally protected. Additionally the Rock Art Foundation has omitted all GPS coordinates of the actual site, thereby, securing the future of the ancient carvings.

Oldest Community

Or, communities?

Approaching the town of Genoa, you're inundated with road signs lining the highway with that oh-so-famous branding of "Nevada's Oldest Settlement." With its ornate courthouse and lovely brick and wooden structures seemingly on display, Genoa would seem worthy of the title. But not all is fair in love and age—at least in the Silver State.

Meanwhile, twenty-five miles to the east, the city of Dayton bites back with signs of its own, solidly fastened to its main street: "Nevada's First Gold Discovery, 1849."

It seems the debate is so touch-and-go that even lifelong Nevadans cannot quite settle on an answer!

Both communities were commercially active during this time, but each of them carried out separate trades at the time in question from 1849 to 1851. The issue, turned fashionable debate, now seems to be based completely on hometown pride and some very questionable facts.

In recent years, many historians have religiously concluded that Dayton wins this pride of prides. And well, the records don't lie!

Early documents show that the earliest "permanent" residents of Dayton were gold-seekers who settled at the mouth of Gold Canyon in the spring of 1851, at least two weeks before settlers had set up shop at Mormon Station (soon to be renamed Genoa the same year). Old "Day-Town" barely took up any room along the Carson River and consisted of a mere hodgepodge of tents, shacks, and makeshift shelters.

Twenty-five miles away and two weeks later, residents at Mormon Station had already plotted land. However, the town sported a well-defined main street and began construction of a courthouse, post office, general store, and several permanent ranches that were already selling product to nearby settlers. This *permanence* could very well be the one-two punch that downs the debate for good.

So, do Nevadans crown this honorable title to a tranquil farming community nestled at the base of the mountains, or do we bestow the honor to a dusty gold mining outpost along the Carson River? It's likely that this friendly quarrel will continue to rattle state residents for years to come. So, sit back and watch the sparks fly, or rather, why not ponder the question inside our next three superlatives?

Oldest Building

You'd expect such a sacred superlative hidden away amongst the hundreds of old towns scattered in the outback of Nevada, or maybe camouflaged along the main streets of Dayton or Virginia City. However, in a state notorious for its old buildings, this one comes as a surprise for most Nevadans.

Many people forget that Las Vegas—a city renowned for its sin and vices—was actually founded by Mormons on June 14, 1855. How's that for shock value?

Thirty Mormon missionaries by order of Brigham Young constructed a 13,070 square foot adobe fort—thereby solidifying the first permanent structure in the Las Vegas Valley. The fort was surrounded by 14-foot high adobe walls, enclosing eight two-story homes for the missionaries along with a full-fledged, but crude, medical facility that provided aid for anybody passing through or inhabiting the valley.

Even though it was called a fort, it was never used for any military troops or purposes; like many Mormon forts, it provided a defense and shelter for local settlers and travelers. Instead, they cultivated small fields and gardens, planted fruit trees, and established friendly relations with the native Southern Paiutes of the area.

In 1857, Brigham Young decided that the Mormon effort of further "growing" the area was a fruitless endeavor, and the fort was abandoned just two years later.

Before the fort's construction, Las Vegas was a barely inhabited blip on the map, but it was seen as a vital watering hole on the trail between Salt Lake City and Los Angeles. Young's fort would forever change the status of this barren little blip. If only he knew what it would become!

> Nevada's Oldest Building is the centerpiece of the Old Las Vegas Mormon Fort State Historic Park, located at 500 E Washington Street in downtown Las Vegas. Rangers at the state park will allow you to visit the museum for free, but there is an entrance fee to explore the actual fort and participate in the park's events and tours. The park is open from 8 a.m. to 4:30 p.m. Tuesday through Saturday. Last admittance is at 4 p.m.

Oldest Hotel

Like a weathered old bird standing from its high perch on the Comstock, the rough-hewn Gold Hill Hotel reigns proudly without peer. Its construction, however, remains a mystery—*sometime* before January 1862.

So what's the deal here? The big uncertainty here lies in the *exact date* on which it was built! Allegedly, the Gold Hill Hotel was actualized in *1862*—a year that's proudly depicted on the hotel's signage for over a century. This date has become a thorn in the side of most state historians, as many will debunk this huge historical blooper without pause.

Looks Good on Paper?

The logic behind using this particular year falls apart quicker than a Comstock mudslide. Records show that the first recorded discovery took place in the early spring of 1859.

In a frenzy to dig out as much silver as possible before the year's-end freezing temperatures, miner's camps needed to be fairly basic; men erected only tents, dugouts, or shacks for shelter. Simply put, 1859 was too early of a time frame for such a substantial building. The sheer time, cost, and dedication of building such a gargantuan hotel seems highly unlikely.

At least "1859" looks damn good on a letterhead!

> Find the Gold Hill Hotel at 1540 S. Main Street in Gold Hill along SR 342, 15 miles north of Carson City. The famous Crown Point Restaurant serves lunch and dinner for 363 days of the year, with reservations recommended during the busy months of October through November, aka Halloween season. Speaking of which, the Gold Hill Hotel comes with its own fanfare if you book a night in one of its immaculate 19th-century rooms. I won't spoil the surprise. Instead, give them a call at (775) 847-0111.

Oldest Saloon

While debate looms over the state's oldest community, the home of Nevada's oldest thirst parlor goes solidly to the Genoa Bar, built in the spring of 1863.

In the minds of Nevadans, this sweet title might just be the very best one.

The Genoa Bar first opened for business as "Livingston's Exchange," and later rebranded as a gentleman's saloon by the name of "Fettic's Exchange" in 1884. Since then, this ol' girl has changed hands several times through the years. Today, the bar still offers up the best beer and bras for miles around—complete with its dusty windows and a unique musk filled in nostalgia.

Ins and Outs at the Genoa Bar

Given its long life, the Genoa Bar has served as an elegant hostess to several historical figures for over a century and a half, boasting a fascinating storyboard of interesting facts. Chug 'em down!

- Mark Twain made regular visits during his reporting for the *Territorial Enterprise* during the 1860s.

- Presidents Ulysses S. Grant and Teddy Roosevelt came through Genoa specifically to down a few cold ones at the bar.

- In the 1930's, Hollywood sweethearts Clark Gable and Carole Lombard visited here to play high stakes poker with the local cattle barons.

- Merle Haggard, John Denver, Charlie Daniels, Waylon Jennings, Willie Nelson, and Johnny Cash all visited the Genoa Bar in search of a bit of inspiration.

- Hollywood left their mark by filming several movies at the bar, including *The Shootist*, *Misery*, *Til' the River Runs Dry*, and *A Place Called Home*.

- In the 1970s, Raquel Welch visited the Genoa Bar and the patrons asked if she could leave her bra. She agreed but insisted that all the other bras hanging in the establishment be taken down! Today, Welch's black leopard print bra still hangs festively on a pair of antlers over the bar top.

- In the late 1840s, the Diamond Dust Mirror, set festively on the back of the bar, originated from Glasgow, Scotland and was brought in a covered wagon from San Francisco. Check out the actual diamonds in the mirror frame!

- If you look closely at the foot of the bar, you'll notice a hidden trap door that conceals a cold storage room used to refrigerate meats and drinks for over a hundred years.

- In the mid 1980s, the Coors Beer Company came here to film a commercial. Unfortunately, the locals hired to be extras didn't like Coors beer. To proceed with filming, Coors allowed them to empty their cans and fill them with their favorite suds.

Oldest Courthouse

148 years and still going strong!

Virginia City's ornate Storey County Courthouse has been operating in Nevada ever since its founding in 1875. Justice is not blind here in Storey County as shown by the judicial statue gracing the front gables of the building. Most courthouses display our lovely Lady of Justice blindfolded, though here in Storey County her eyes are wide open.

Maybe it's because of the fantastic view?

The massive courthouse serves a tiny population centered in only two areas of the county—the Comstock (a colloquial name for the communities of Virginia City and Gold Hill) and the town of Lockwood on the north bank of the Truckee River. However, the Comstock and Lockwood are separated by over forty miles of uninhabited mountains. This means that to keep law and order, Storey sheriffs have to travel long distances on winding roads to get across the county!

One local sheriff gruffly told me how they make it work: *It's gotta get done.*

Although it's acted as the longest-serving courthouse in Nevada, it is not the oldest. The Douglas County courthouse—built in 1865—lost its status as the longest-running after moving from Genoa to Minden in 1916.

Oldest Gaming License

What began as a simple roadside saloon now celebrates a lifetime of nearly 95 years. We're talking about Nevada's oldest gaming establishment which you'll find atop Railroad Pass in between Henderson and Boulder City.

"The Pass" as it's affectionately known, was built during the height of Prohibition and construction of the Hoover Dam in 1931. The town of Boulder City had outlawed both gaming and alcohol and the little bar atop Railroad Pass provided a bit of a fix and nightlife for the lonely dam workers.

> Wait! Couldn't the Genoa Bar qualify as the state's oldest casino?

> What exactly separates a casino from a hotel or a bar that allows gaming?

So glad you asked!

"Casino" refers to *an establishment built specifically for gaming in which a gaming license is required*. The Genoa Bar was built primarily for other purposes: a bar.

For example, this superlative had a huge contender with the Commercial Inn in Elko, originally named the Humboldt Lodging House.

However, note the name.

The Humboldt was originally built to be...a hotel, a building for the purpose of providing accommodation, not for gaming. It wasn't until Nevada legalized gambling in 1931 that owners changed the name to the "Commercial Casino" to draw in gaming. This little detail will no doubt disappoint fans of older buildings like the Old Washoe Club, the Mizpah, or some of the classic multi-stories in Reno and Vegas, such as the Riverside and the Aladdin.

Sorry, Elko. Better luck next time.

In Nevada these terms are sometimes used interchangeably, such as "hotel-casino," and telling them apart can be a little confusing. Here, the Railroad Pass holds THE STATE'S LONGEST ACTIVE GAMING LICENSE and yes...was built solely for the purpose of gaming.

Oldest Brothel

In a state where anything goes, the world's oldest profession has been alive and well since the days of the Old West. The state's first brothels date back to the early mining days of 19th century Nevada—a place where tired men could go for some companionship.

Since then, brothels have become somewhat of a mainstay here in the Silver State, though there still isn't talk of these houses of ill repute without turning a few heads. It wasn't until after the Civil War that the sale of sex was banned throughout the country. However, being the renegade that she is, our state was a holdout and brothels were openly "tolerated" if not explicitly allowed for over fifty years.

Today, only ten of seventeen counties allow prostitution, and only within state-licensed brothels. State law bans brothels in counties with populations of 400,000 or more (currently Clark and Washoe counties) and individual counties have the right to relinquish altogether while implementing their own additional rules.

Ironically, just eight miles east of Carson City, the Silver State's reign of government, you'll find the lavish Moonlite BunnyRanch, the STATE'S OLDEST BROTHEL - FIRST OPENING IN 1955.

The ranch operated discreetly until the 1970s, when Nevada began regulation of prostitution houses. The Moonlite is famous for being featured on a few cable network specials, even leading to a two season television series on HBO. The show brought to light the actual running of a Nevada brothel, once thought to be a shady and dangerous practice, when in fact the truth is no more than another business simply offering services to people.

HIGHEST & LOWEST

Buckle in while we drive your imagination up the High and Mighty Hidden Gems of old Battle Born! Not bad for a state that's said to be *just desert*, eh?

Highest Point

FLOATING ABOVE THE REST of Nevada at 13,140 feet above sea level, the highest of our state's superlatives lingers just ¾ of a mile inside the state line in lonely Esmeralda County.

Boundary Peak is located quite far from most of the state's population in west-central Nevada, pretty much in between nowhere and nowhere and requiring at least a few hours of traveling from any direction. Second, unlike Hood or Rainier, Boundary Peak falls short of dominating the skyline, instead blending in with neighboring peaks. It's no surprise that relatively few Nevadans know about their state's highest point.

Psst. Can you spot Nevada's Highest Point?

In recent years, NDOT has helped things along by installing a huge picnic area with signage soliciting its presence from US 6. Even so you'll need to play a bit of eye-spy as you drop down from Montgomery Pass.

Look to the left at that double peak scraping the sky. Boundary is the furthest left point: a sub-ridge of California's Montgomery Peak.

Summiting Boundary Peak

In 2009, the newly-formed Boundary Peak WIlderness insured that visitors would forever reach the top of Nevada without too much trouble. However, getting to the top is a feat that should be attempted only by the most accomplished hikers. A typical conquering of Boundary Peak involves a long, grueling slug from the desert floor via Trail Canyon—an ascent that takes about seven hours.

The safest time to summit Boundary is late June through early October. Make the plan to summit by late morning and plan to be off the ridge by late afternoon to avoid the range's nasty t-storms. In the summer, the White Mountains create their own nefarious weather patterns famous for chasing hikers off the mountain by its wild summer lightning!

OH YEAH. BRAGGING RIGHTS WILL BE IN ORDER FOR BAGGING THE TALLEST POINT IN THE MOST MOUNTAINOUS STATE IN THE UNITED STATES.

> From SR 264, look for a road signed to "Trail Canyon, Boundary Peak" about 20 miles south of US 6, or 74 miles southwest of Tonopah. Follow this road for five miles to Trail Canyon Reservoir at 6,340 feet. A wooden sign and trailhead for Boundary Peak Wilderness sits at the road's end. Do some fishing, make camp, and start for the summit early the next morning. The road continues past the reservoir, but only foot traffic is allowed past the wilderness boundary. This path is an 8-mile slug up to the summit. Allow at least 8-10 hours via this route. Bring plenty of water and sunscreen as shade will be non-existent for the majority of the torturous path.

Highest Paved Road

Perhaps no drive better exemplifies what Nevada and its Great Basin are all about than the fabulous ride up the Snake Range via the Wheeler Peak Scenic Byway.

This bad boy was fashioned in 1946 long before the establishment of Great Basin National Park. Visitors to what was then Lehman Caves National Monument adored this drive so much that the Scenic Drive became the unofficial poster child upon the park's dedication in 1986.

The Scenic Drive begins at 7,000 feet in a thick pinyon pine forest, wasting no time in ascending some 3,000 feet above the desert floor in just 12 miles. The road ends just shy of the tree line at Wheeler Peak Campground at 10,240 feet, a mere 800 feet lower than the first grove of Bristlecone Pines!

Along the way, the cliff-hugging course unveils a handful of inspiring, hundred-mile views and dramatically changing ecosystems as it ascends the range, from sagebrush ocean, to pinyon pine forest, to mountain mahogany, to dark witchy woods of pines and firs.

This is a legitimate crash course in Great Basin topography.

Four Seasons on the Scenic Byway

But why not trade four wheels for two? The 12 mile bike ride up the Scenic Byway is a creaky knees endurance marathon turned hair-raising roller-coaster ride on the way down. Top if off with air whipping in your face as you soak in the marvelous views before you—one that challenges your wits as you try to keep your eyes on the twists and turns.

If you have a full day and legs as powerful as a Bobcat (the plow, not the cat!) you can also cross-country ski all the way to the top of the 12 mile path. Snowshoeing the scenic drive has become a popular pilgrimage marketed by the National Park Service—an adventure that pretty much guarantees one of the most solitary experiences in the country.

So, how about it? Why not tackle the highest paved road in the only national park in Nevada?

Highest Mountain Range

Out of all 315 named mountain ranges in the state (not to mention the hundreds of unnamed ones!), the White Mountains come out on top.

Quite literally.

The White Mountains stand true as not only THE HIGHEST RANGE IN NEVADA, BUT THE ENTIRE GREAT BASIN ITSELF. Averaging 10,663 feet above sea level, this fantastical island range reaches sixty incredible miles and rears a dominating presence in the remote barrens of central Nevada and eastern California.

You'll find that eight of these peaks throughout both states exceed 10,000 feet (including our state's highest point) with enough snowmelt to feed twenty-six perennial streams and two hundred endemic species.

And well, if you find yourself cruising US 95 near Tonopah in the spring, you'll see how the range acquired its name.

The bobbing Whites resemble clouds floating high above empty salt pans and barren salt scrub desert. But their remote location is far from most of the state's population; sadly, it's a sight that few Nevadans will see.

The White Mountains are most famed as the home of the Ancient Bristlecone Pine Forest, twenty-six miles east of Big Pine. Even though it's just one of the many ranges that harbor the world's oldest things, the Bristlecones that live here are the most numerous, and arguably the most picturesque, in the world.

> Only two paved highways (US 6 and CA 168) actually cross the White Mountains, but dozens of side canyons up perennial streams call for perfect, but rugged, access into its heart from the east. Among these will be Indian Creek, Chiatovich Creek, Furnace Creek, Trail Canyon from Fish Lake Valley (SR 264), and of course, the trail up to Boundary Peak, the state's highest point. These trips will require four-wheel-drive and some spare essentials.

You'll find better access in the Golden State from the *White Mountains Scenic Byway*, a 12-mile long dreamy drive from CA 168 into the Ancient Bristlecone Pine Forest. From here, you can access Patriarch and Methuselah Groves of Bristlecone Pine at the very top of the range, as well as some remote pockets of paradise like Cottonwood Basin and Silver Creek. If you have the lungs for it, the rigorous 5-hour climb to White Mountain Peak (14,252') is a supreme destination in itself as the third highest peak in California, fifth in the Great Basin, and the highest in the Whites. Holy superlative!

World's Highest Concrete Arch Bridge

Fully named the *Mike O'Callaghan–Pat Tillman Memorial Bridge*, this beast spans 1,060 feet wide, 1,900 feet long, and soars 912 feet above the Colorado River. Yup, Mike O' Pat Bridge, or simply the Hoover Dam Bridge, is the tallest bridge in Nevada, the second highest bridge in the U.S., and THE WORLD'S HIGHEST CONCRETE ARCHED BRIDGE.

Not bad for a *dam* bridge.

Mike O' Pat opened in 2010 as the key component of the Hoover Dam Bypass—a lengthy project that rerouted thru-traffic onto its own bridge spanning the Colorado River into Arizona. This amazing engineering feat also incorporates the widest concrete arch in the Western Hemisphere.

Oh, but let's slather it on more! The Mike O' Pat is also the first concrete and steel composite bridge built in the United States with <u>USA Today</u> even calling it "America's Newest Wonder." How's that for a few titles?

> FROM BOULDER CITY, FOLLOW INTERSTATE 11/US 93 SOUTH FOR 4 MILES TO THE "LAST NEVADA EXIT." Here, you'll find a frontage road with an awesome view of the bridge spanning the deep chasm of the Colorado River. (This road also leads to the Hoover Dam touring area and the "old road" over the dam.) From the Arizona side, you'll find a truck parking area with added views of the Hoover Dam generators along with the famous "Pacific Time Zone" sign.

Highest Mountain Pass

At 8,900 feet, Mt. Rose Summit on SR 431 is so high in elevation that snow lingers on the shoulders well into July.

> What? Snow in July?

You bet, and you are in a betting state.

Expecting snow and inclement weather at any time of the year on 431 is not being overly prudent at all, but mindful in the ways of the local.

Whenever you're in doubt, take a gander at the twelve-foot tall snow markers that line the highway as you swivel and snake up the mountainside. As you progress further up the mountain, it's always a feast for the eyes when Mount Rose's giant monolith suddenly breaks through the forest.

Highest Historical Site

If you find yourself set deep in the wilds near the center of the state, you might stumble upon a little-known secret called Alta Toquima—THE HIGHEST HISTORICAL SITE, and technically, the highest ghost town in Nevada.

That's exactly what happened in 1978 when Dr. David Thomas of the American Natural Museum stumbled upon what is the highest known Native American Village in all of North America—unearthed here in Nevada on the slopes of the Table Mountains.

Before surveys and excavations actually occurred at Alta Toquima, Dr. Thomas and his team hypothesized that early North American hunters avoided high altitude environments, claiming them as too harsh and barren to sustain life. Archaeologists had previously identified small, temporary base camps as high as 11,000 feet, but they showed no indication of long-term settlement.

In 1980, Dr. Thomas proved otherwise.

Beginning around 2,500 BP through year 0, he learned that small groups of hunters had seasonally harvested mountain sheep here in the Table Mountains, and not long after, he discovered that high altitude villages were well under construction and later occupied by families for months at a time.

These long-term settlements at Alta Toquima represented a major shift in how ancient Americans used mountain resources, furthermore illustrating how archaeological research continues to teach us about the past.

Into the Wilds of Alta Toquima

Make no mistake. Do not attempt to visit this site if you lack skills in self-sufficiency and extreme back-country travel!

The village itself is located on the south slope of Mt. Jefferson's North Summit (11,946'), a long day's hike to the northwest from the trailhead. It's imperative that you manage your time well so you're not caught by freak lightning storms in the summer, and you're back down at a lower elevation before deathly freezing temperatures come at nightfall.

> THE REMOTE VILLAGE OF ALTA TOQUIMA IS ABOUT AS INHOSPITABLE AS IT GETS. What remains of the village is located on a very steep slope at over 11,000 feet. Nothing comes easy here because finding the village site requires a long, detailed slug on foot or on horseback. Stock up on all provisions in Tonopah and retreat 82 miles—don't worry, you can do this part in a car!—east to the small mining town of Belmont. Your trip has only just begun. From here, follow the unpaved Belmont Road (Sometimes signed as "Monitor Valley Road"/"Old SR 82") into Monitor Valley for 33 miles. Here, a sign marks the way to "Table Mountain Wilderness, Pine Creek." Turn here and continue up Pine Creek Canyon for about 7 miles to a small campground. This lonely camp is your trailhead into the very remote Table Mountain Wilderness and home to the highest elevation Native American village in North America. The route to Alta Toquima is unmarked, so please procure the best topo maps you can find! Use the latest Humboldt-Toiyabe, Table Mountain, Tonopah District maps slated for at least the latest 2023 publication dates.

Highest Lake

© Shutterstock/Peter Silverman

The ramblings don't come easy deep in the back-country of Great Basin National Park. If you're one of the determined few who extend the effort to get here, you'll be rewarded to the stunning shorelines of a glacial bowl named Johnson Lake—the coveted holder for THE HIGHEST LAKE IN NEVADA.

Trust me. Tracking down the highest lake was no easy task, but elevation does not lie.

Start by tracking down the 12.9-mile Baker-Johnson Loop and you'll find a circuitous trail that leads from the east flank of Pyramid Peak to Baker Creek Campground just south of the Lehman Caves Visitor Center.

At the halfway point on the loop, you'll reach this beautiful blue bowl at a whopping 10,800 feet. Pick up your jaw here. After a bit of fly-fishing and general sojourning, you can hit up Nevada's 2nd highest lake by coursing north on the Baker

Lake Trail Loop to nearby Baker Lake (10,620') via a long, but magical ten-mile stroll back to civilization.

Although the entire trek from end-to-end can be done in one day, you'd really be robbing yourself from really experiencing this mountain majesty. A better option would be a two-day journey: hike up, camp overnight at Johnson or Baker, and then work your way back down Baker Creek the next day for a charming, weekend adventure. The trail to Johnson Lake is clearly marked as it follows an old jeep road up the mountain from either end.

Before making the trip, please inform the rangers at Lehman Caves of your itinerary. This is solely for safety in this remote park without many visitors.

> YOU CAN BEST REACH JOHNSON LAKE FROM THE SNAKE CREEK TRAILHEAD. From the town of Baker, head south on SR 487 for 3 miles to the National Park turnoff to *"Snake Creek Canyon."* Turn right here and continue 10 miles back into the park. Although the National Park Service has made sure Snake Creek Road remains open to all vehicles, they like to keep it as primitive as possible, therefore making the 10 miles seem like 25. The road ends at the Baker-Johnson Loop trailhead inside a lovely meadow at 8,600 feet with a looming view of Pyramid Peak.

Highest & Lowest Recorded Temperatures

THE HOTTEST TEMPERATURE EVER RECORDED IN NEVADA OCCURRED IN LAUGHLIN ON JUNE 29, 1994—TIPPING THE MERCURY AT *125°F!*

This monster reading was a result of an excessive heatwave that stormed through the American Southwest affecting cities throughout Arizona, Utah, California, and Nevada. It's predicted that roaring heat waves such as these occur only once every ten years, though it has never again been recorded at such a height.

On the opposite end of the scale (and opposite end of the state), THE COLDEST TEMPERATURE EVER RECORDED IN NEVADA WAS -50°F, OCCURRING AT SAN JACINTO RANCH ON JANUARY 8, 1937.

While it isn't uncommon for northern Nevada to reach temperatures below zero, dropping down below -10° is considered a little unusual. At the time, San Jacinto was a somewhat quiet outpost, operating a natural spring, and general store between Wells and Twin Falls. Records show that the shopkeeper had closed his store in preparation for an incoming blizzard, and he couldn't have done it at a better time.

Only about two inches of snow fell that day, but the temperature alone was enough to shut down all transportation for the following three days. That wintry incident has since been Nevada's lowest state record for the last 88 years.

Lowest Point

While the state's highest point can be reached with some effort, the same might not be said of the state's lowest point.

At just 479 feet above sea level, Nevada's lowest point is an epic meeting of three states at the bottom of the Colorado River. Coincidentally, it also carries the unusual distinction of also being one of Nevada's 5 tri-state points. That's right, five! Let's do this.

The closest the average Nevadan will get to visiting this locale will most likely be at Big Bend of the Colorado State Recreation Area, which sits about 4 miles north of the actual lowest point. Big Bend boasts a measly elevation of 500 feet above sea level. If you're unsatisfied with this "almost" low point of Big Bend, you're going to have to get your feet wet to reach the actual lowest point.

To get to the very bottom of Nevada, and coincidentally, the state's lowest point, start in Laughlin and head south on Needles Highway. After crossing into California (approximately 7 miles from SR 163), turn left onto Aha Macav Parkway and follow the road for 2 miles to join up with Aztec Road at the Avi Resort & Casino.

Now you can put some gravel in your travel.

Just before crossing the Colorado River, turn onto an unsigned and unpaved road with a gate heading south along the river. Sometimes this gate is closed per the Mohave Reservation, so please be respectful.

After 0.4 miles you'll arrive at a large pullout at the CA/NV state line. Your careful eyes may spot the actual state line running through the road. Look to the left. The exact lowest point of Nevada is approximately 130 feet into the river.

Congratulations.

You've not only reached the lowest point in Nevada, but also the farthest south you can get in the Silver State, and one of only a handful of tri-state points in the country. Thumbs up to this cool superlative!

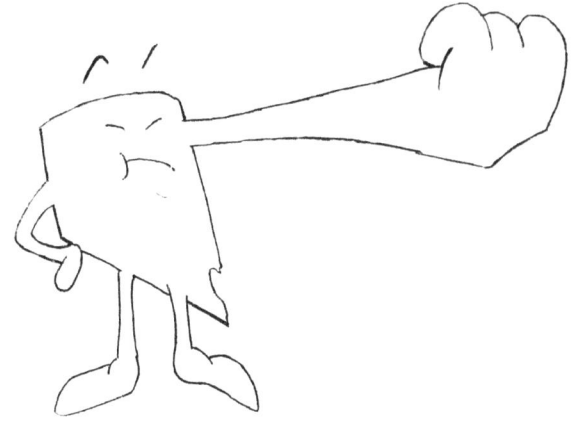

LONGEST & SHORTEST

Here's to the long and short of our state's supers with no straws drawn too short here. Enjoy these fascinating–and sometimes weird— wonderful winners of this peppy title.

Shortest Highway

OH, LITTLE 781. YOU'RE PROOF THAT SIZE DOESN'T MATTER.

This little guy consists of a single bridge over the Humboldt River at the town site of Palisade in the northern panhandle of Eureka County. It almost seems like a joke, but no, this is an actual state highway, built and maintained by the NDOT.

The entirety of State Route 781 measures a whopping 332 feet, or 0.063 miles, and has no connection to any other highway in the state. Considering that the only thing of significance out here is the river, it begs the question: why this highway was designated in the first place?

A single gravel road leads to Palisade from SR 278, only briefly interrupted by the paved highway (and bridge) over the river before continuing its gravel journey!

This area is so isolated that the demand for a full-fledged, state-funded highway bridge in the middle of nowhere is equally fascinating and confusing.

Couldn't there just be a bridge without the need for a highway designation?

Either way, throw your hands up for this double superlative. The next time you're in north central Nevada, why not cross the state's longest river on the state's shortest highway? The silence out here and the wildlife echoing in the canyon will be worth the trip alone. Be here for an amazing day's end at one of the state's most beautiful sundown locations.

> State Route 781 is nigh-impossible to find on any map or road atlas, so we're helping you out here.
> Start by leaving Interstate 80 on Exit 289 for SR 278 signed south to Eureka. Continue on SR 278 for approximately 9.1 miles to unsigned Palisade Ranch Road. (You'll find this road just south of Historical Marker #65.) Turn right here and continue another 1.5 miles toward the river. The bridge before you is SR 781 and NEVADA'S SHORTEST HIGHWAY.

For the road geeks out there, you're so welcome.

Longest Road

At almost seven hundred miles long (665.835 miles), US 95 is the vital backbone for Nevada, one that loosely connects the state's two mega cities with each other—even binding the northern and southern portions of our great state together.

This lengthy beast, known as the "Silver Trails Highway," is a mostly two-lane route that crosses into Nevada from Oregon at the tiny gateway town of McDermitt and hightails it to the very southern tip of the state before crossing into California some 72 miles south of Las Vegas. Along the way, commuters often associate *The 95* with dozens of long, "empty" stretches of desert, broken up only by small communities in between the two mega cities of Reno and Las Vegas.

Longest-Running Show

Every year in Sin City alone, at least a handful of "longest-running" shows headline marquees and billboards along the 15, and well, most of these are marketing ploys for specific resorts. Thanks to the non-stagnant enterprises in both Reno and Las Vegas over the past sixty years, this superlative has had a few close contenders, but like any decent run here, there must be only one winner.

The Tropicana in Las Vegas proudly boasts three of the Strip's longest-running shows, but only *Folies Bergere* truly wins the number one spot.

Running since 1959, longer than any other production on the Strip, *Folies Bergere* showcases a French-style topless number that thrills some 40,000 fans every month, dazzling the bobbing heads of audience members from around the world.

Folies offers a glimpse at some of the award-winning musical numbers from past shows along with fantastic new pieces in its later years. The revue eventually evolved into a true variety show with singing, dancing, spectacular sets, and beautiful showgirls.

Think classic Las Vegas entertainment and you can easily picture this glamorous production—a timeless musical extravaganza that embodies the very essence of rebellious, golden-era Las Vegas entertainment.

Longest Lived Mining Camp

Mining camps are a dime-a-dozen little treasures throughout our state's history-- most with snarky names like Bullion, Gold Hit, Weepah, Black Horse, and my personal favorite: Leadfoot. Some were prosperous. Others were flash-in-the-pan camps lucky to survive a year.

AND THEN THERE'S PIOCHE.

This little silver city in Lincoln County has earned its status as the longest-lived mining camp in Nevada, operating for an astounding 160 years.

Rough and Tumble

The story of Pioche *(pronounced "PIE-ohsh")* begins in 1864 like many others in the Silver State: men digging hard and fast with little to show for it until the very last minute. By 1872, Pioche had organized itself into a full-fledged city of six thousand residents after a silver buzz brought forth a wild rush of fortune seekers.

Pioche became a breeding ground for tough gunmen and bitter lawsuits. In fact, it even earned the reputation as one of the roughest towns in the West, headlining newspapers and rivaling camps in Arizona, Colorado, and Wyoming as the roughest, toughest... and bloodiest!

Local lore claims that seventy-five men were killed by a lead slug before the first natural death ever occurred in town.

Its legend has been immortalized by many of the headstones on "Boot Hill"--- a compelling cemetery in town that catalogs those who met their fateful end staring down the barrel of a gun or feeling the sharp end of a blade.

Little Pioche has refused to give up the ghost and while sporadic mining still carries on, the now-quaint burg plays out its important role in Nevada today as the Lincoln County seat. Today, visitors will find Boot Hill's interesting homage to the town's rough and tumble past, and a pretty little city far from most of Nevada's civilization, rife with a main street straight out of an Old West memoir.

Longest Urban Street

When the NDOT paved the original 1860s wagon route, it's likely they had no idea that it cemented Virginia Street as THE LONGEST URBAN STREET IN THE STATE. The entire 28.630-mile length of Virginia Street owes its existence to its direct connection with nearby California. In fact, it's possible to drive to the state line entirely on Virginia without ever setting foot on the freeway as the whole complex winds, then pokes along through Reno and Truckee Meadows.

So, what can you expect on an every day, but never dull amble down Nevada's longest street?

 North Virginia Street

North Virginia officially begins at Exit 38 along US 395 at Red Rock Road, 8 miles north of Reno where it runs south to McCarran Boulevard, 1.5 miles north of the downtown strip. However, an unpaved road (the original wagon route) continues north from Red Rock Road to the California state line at Bordertown. Interestingly, NDOT still signs this old wagon route as "Virginia Street", which theoretically can add even more mileage to this listing!

 Virginia Street

Once hitting downtown, North Virginia turns into the Virginia Street we all know and love.

After McCarran Boulevard, Virginia Street heads south past the University of Nevada and becomes the Reno Strip— the neon jungle of northern Nevada. This portion of Virginia is synonymous with many of the highlights of the region, such as the Reno Arch, Hot August Nights, Reno Midtown, and the famous Wedding Band Bridge over the Truckee River. After leaving downtown, Virginia meets up once again with the loop of McCarran Boulevard halfway through urban Reno near Meadowood Mall.

[3] *South Virginia Street*

From here, Virginia Street turns into South Virginia Street where it gradually grows in size to a four-lane route as it enters Damonte Ranch. Here, it meets a busy intersection with Mt. Rose Highway (SR 431) and Geiger Grade (SR 341).

[4] *Old US 395*

South Virginia Street continues past the Rose/Geiger intersection onto the route of US 395 ALT. Most locals know this as "Old 395," even though the route is still designated as *South Virginia*. By any name, this scenic little back road ambles through a shallow valley where it meets its official end—11 miles later in Washoe Valley, right in the shadow of Slide Mountain and the Carson Range.

Versus Las Vegas Boulevard

When researching for this book, we originally thought The Las Vegas Strip would be the obvious winner here, but it came just shy of winning this title with *25.111 miles*.

We painstakingly tracked the route's official designation as *"Las Vegas Boulevard"* proper from the Apex interchange (Exit 58) all the way south to Jean (Exit 12) along I-15 from beginning to end. This was so close that had the designation for *"Las Vegas Blvd"* continued north or south from any of its two endpoints, this superlative might have gone to the South.

Longest Continuous Unpaved Road

Nevada is a state inundated with more gravel roads than perhaps anywhere else in the lower 48. In fact, with some careful planning it is still possible to travel entirely north to south or east to west across the state solely on dirt roads.

In this case, the definition of "continuous" we are using means *one length*, and *one single road* from end to end with *no shared routes* or intermittency. After some careful research, thorough BLM map comparisons, and obsessive phone calls, we've concluded that OLD STATE ROUTE 8A TRAVELS THE LONGEST CONTINUOUS DISTANCE OF ANY UNPAVED ROAD IN THE SILVER STATE.

8A is the only east-west through route in the "Northwest Corner," a *200-square mile* sector of Nevada with no services and a population of less than 150 residents in total.

Into the Outback of Nevada

8A begins as a remote continuation of California Highway 299 just east of Cedarville. Here, you're met with an ominous, weathered sign that reads *"No Emergency Services in Northern Washoe County."*

8A then undulates over lofty hills to the outpost of Vya: the region's only "major" crossroads.

At this point, the adventure unfolds as the road barrels its way into nowhere heading northeast through the Sheldon National Wildlife Refuge to intersect with SR 140, grinding along at a total distance of 123.6 miles!

Aside from a handful of ranches and BLM back-country shelters, the northwest corner is one of the last places left where society hasn't quite taken hold. The BLM graciously warns travelers at both ends of the route that winter travel is prohibited because of the region's immense isolation. In 1993, 8A nearly consumed the Stolpa family who found themselves stranded during the winter, bottoming out in two feet of snow, succumbing to frostbite, dehydration, and starvation—hundreds of miles from any form of help.

A trip on 8A should be met with celebration as very few people will ever have the privilege or wherewithal to experience this awesome back-country byway.

Longest Cathedral-Arch Bridge in the World

Now you're probably thinking ...

> "Um, you already mentioned that the biggest bridge was the Hoover Dam Bridge!"

True. However, we could argue this: the Hoover Dam Bridge is shared between two states and therefore is *not fully contained within Nevada*. The Galena Creek Bridge, however, answers this conundrum and arguably, could be the end-all winner to the title.

A less complicated reason to include Galena Creek would be this: it's a completely different type of bridge that deserves its own section separate from its predecessor. See, Galena Creek is classified as a "cathedral arch" bridge, which has no columns going from the arch itself up to the superstructure, AKA, the flat part people drive on. If you look at photos of both bridges, you can see columns rising out of the arch at Hoover Dam but not at Galena Creek.

Piqued your curiosity? Time to break down this bad boy.

At 1,725 feet long and over 300 feet tall, the Galena Creek Bridge is the centerpiece of the state's largest transportation project, encompassing an 8.5-mile long freeway extension of Interstate 580 that connects Reno and Carson City with an improved freeway system.

The unique design of this bridge was not only drafted for aesthetics, but more to safely accommodate commuters over the area's topsy-turvy terrain and famously high winds, many of which exceed 50 miles per hour. Years of careful planning and intuitive design were essential to preserve the natural habitat of Galena Creek while providing a safe and speedy freeway connection for the area.

© *Donna Kennedy*

Additionally, designers specifically gave the bridge huge aesthetic appeal per request of Pleasant Valley residents who feared the new interstate would intrude on their unobstructed mountain view. They implemented a lovely double-arch structure which now seems to compliment the glistening slopes of Mt. Rose in the background.

If you want a one-of-a-kind bridge in Nevada (even if it *is* in a rare category with few competitors), the winner goes to Galena Creek: *the world's longest cathedral arch bridge.*

Case closed.

Longest Mountain Range

Nevada publications tend to be saturated with images highlighting Wheeler Peak and the Snake Range, Lake Tahoe and its famed Tahoe Rim Trail, or the shimmering gold hillsides of the Ruby Mountains. Perhaps the powers-that-be refuse to acknowledge the majestic, and often overlooked, Schell Creek Range.

Or maybe they just haven't found their way here yet.

This mountain chain, known colloquially as the "Schells," stretches for approximately 132 miles in an almost perfect north-south line, comprising two major groups of peaks commonly viewed as the North and South Schells.

This range of glory covers a length longer than the state of Delaware–-with plenty of room to spare.

Be Schell, My Heart!

The Schell's highest point at North Schell Peak (11,880') sits in tandem with Taft and South Schell Peaks— a mighty trio that collectively wrings out over eighty inches of precipitation every year. What appears as a huge monolith of dry mountains from the valley floors suddenly becomes a lush island carpeted in fir forests, riparian canyons, aspen groves, and massive wildflower meadows. Twenty-two perennial streams flow both west and east of the range with dozens of side canyons providing moderate to challenging access into its higher reaches.

In 2021, guestbooks and trailhead sheets concluded that less than a thousand people had ventured into the Schells. The downside (or upside, depending on your perspective) is that there are no extensive trail systems. All access into the range is generally done via the canyons, and from there, mountain hopping or cross-country travel to prominent landmarks.

In time, this massive mountain range may be discovered by young and old Nevadans alike, but for now, those who do know about it whisper quietly about a secret, magical place. While they may not graze the covers of illustrious books or magazines (yet), the Schells best represent a raw, robust, and ravishing wild Nevada.

> THE MOST POPULAR ROUTE INTO THE SCHELL CREEK RANGE IS UNDENIABLY THE SUCCESS SUMMIT LOOP, a 34-mile beauty that hugs the mountains to and from US 93 north and south of Ely. However, backcountry access into the Schell Creek Range requires a bit more planning, but every minute you spend buried in a topo map will be worth it.
>
> Use SR 893 for the range's rugged east slope and US 93 and the paved Duck Valley Road for the west slope. Hikers can access the South Schells via Cleve Creek Campground from the east, or from Berry Creek Campground from the west. Any of the streams on the range's steeper east side teem with wild trout and provide a fairly easy, but long, day trip out of Ely. Aside from Connors Pass (US 6/50/93), the only access over the range is the horrible road along Kalamazoo Creek in the North Schells, but given its extensive venture into the mountains, provides the best way for those with a sturdy rig.

Longest Valley

If viewed from above, the Reese River Valley resembles a stretched-out funnel north to south, averaging about ten miles in width, but fanning out to over twenty-five miles near Battle Mountain. It's easy to find on any map of Central Nevada: a broad and massive sea of sagebrush stretching for 153 miles from the Humboldt River to the historic town of Ione. Find yourself here, and it would take you three and a half hours to drive the valley from end to end.

Uh-huh. Guess how we know this?

On the west side, the Reese is absorbed into several high spots and ridges, yet meets an abrupt end at the walls of the Toiyabe Range on the east. In fact, one of the most iconic scenes of the American West has to be the dramatic view of the valley's backdrop against the bobbing snow-capped Toiyabes as you drop down on US 50 from the west.

The 130-mile-long Reese River runs up the center of the valley originating in the mountains as a freestone stream and crawling the valley floor as a brown muddy course. In the early 1860s at the height of Austin's fantastic mining boom, sneaky mining corporations managed to pull in a bit of easy money from eager, yet gullible east coast investors by marketing the "Reese River Navigation Company."

This is no Mississippi! Instead, the Reese River was nothing more than a muddy, pathetic rivulet, much as it is today. In most years the Reese dwindles into shallow pools long before it ever makes it to the north valley.

Longest Stretch of Road Without Services

In a state known for its empty roads and wide expanses, one could attach this title to just about every other lonely ribbon of highway in Nevada. In this case, one particular blacktop conquers them all.

Much like a tight belt, US 6 connects Nevada east and west across the waist of the state, and the portion of highway between Ely and Tonopah (lovingly nicknamed "the ghost stretch") is THE LONGEST SECTION OF PAVED ROAD WITHOUT SERVICES IN THE ENTIRE STATE.

Upon leaving Ely or Tonopah, you won't find a single form of services for approximately *168.330 miles.*

This barren and mostly lawless highway may serve as a rite of passage for not only Nevadans, but general Loneliness Seekers who relish in getting away from civilization. In 2023, NDOT concluded an average daily traffic count of only 330 vehicles on US 6, and a whopping 220 vehicles per day on the "ghost stretch."

"America's Loneliest Road?" Meh.

Ah, US 50. Nevada's biggest cash grab outside of Las Vegas.

Most Nevadans are familiar with the common quip given to US Highway 50 by Life Magazine in 1996. The famous article denotes that people who choose to drive the route across Nevada need to put their "survival skills" to the test. Rather than taking it like a pejorative, the State of Nevada celebrated the route's loneliness via magazine columns and travel guides.

You'd be hard pressed *not* to find something about the highway inside any welcome center in the state. Today, you can even pick up your own "Highway 50 Survival Kit" in the towns of Fallon, Austin, Eureka, and Ely and get your "survival" stamped by the governor himself.

Challenge accepted— but, let's shatter the bubble.

According to NDOT data, US 50 is far from the "loneliest road" in Nevada. Compare the number above with 50's average daily traffic count of 1,658 vehicles per day over the length of three counties.

On an interesting note, US 6 barely beats the second-place winner for this title by only *1.86 miles*: State Route 375, or more famously named, the "Extraterrestrial Highway." Approximately halfway on this route, the highway comes within ten miles of the alleged Area 51.

Longest River

At 330 miles, and the second longest river in the Great Basin, Nevada's longest river, might also be the state's most important waterway. Through its hundreds of tributaries, the Humboldt furnishes the only natural transportation artery across the Great Basin.

The serpentine Humboldt begins at a site known as Humboldt Wells at a convergence with the T and Marys River in northeastern Elko County. Its long life is unceremoniously cut short at the edge of the dreaded "Forty Mile Desert" in the Humboldt Sink. This pathetic ending of the river almost mimics, if not greatly symbolizes the history that played out along its banks more than 150 years ago.

Following in the Way of Yester Year

"The Humbug" was perhaps the cruelest joke that nature had ever played on the westward emigrants in the 1850s. Emigrants and their oxen soon tired of its hard, brackish water halfway along their journey through Nevada en route to California's fantastical goldfields.

However, the Humboldt proved to be a necessity. Despite the river's difficult surroundings, no other waterway provided a more direct route across the barrens of northern Nevada.

The Humboldt River provided such a reliable route that upon its construction in 1952, the section of Interstate 80 through Nevada was built so that it roughly paralleled the river's lazy slog for more than 250 miles across the state. Today, the river's course still determines the quickest route from Salt Lake City to Reno across Nevada. Love it or hate it, the Humbug is a true travelers' companion here in ol' Battle Born.

LARGEST & SMALLEST

What else can we say about our grandest superlatives? If bigger is better, then these go-getters seize it! Many of these supers showboat even some hefty world-wide stats. Anyone up for a very meaty or pint-sized bow?

Largest Payout

IN 2008, A 25-YEAR-OLD software engineer from Los Angeles won an unfathomable $38.7 million, a payout that to this day set the record for THE LARGEST SLOT PAYOUT IN NEVADA HISTORY. The winner, whose name was not released at request, won this ridiculous sum after popping in just three $1 coins into a Megabucks machine.

The Megabucks system works via interconnected dollar slot machines in approximately 157 casinos throughout Nevada. Generally, the progressive Megabucks Jackpot is paid in equal amounts over 25 years and winners can negotiate other types of payouts. Fortunately for him, the jackpot had been building for seven months after a woman at Bally's Hotel-Casino won a measly $22.6 million.

That'll do, folks.

Largest Alpine Lake in the World

In 1842, John C. Frémont was the first non-native to see Lake Tahoe. In his journals, he remarked: *"Sweet magnificence. A lake of the sky."*

In his writings and ramblings, Mark Twain proclaimed it: *"The greatest view the earth affords."*

And well, we just call it: *Simply magical.*

With its immensity, its clarity, and deep blue inspiration, Lake Tahoe is a place replete of juicy superlatives.

Sixth in the Nation

Lake Tahoe is a massive body of water some 22 miles long by 12 miles wide, totaling 191 square miles. This makes Tahoe the largest alpine lake in the world and the sixth largest lake in the United States. By definition, the word *"alpine"* refers to any lake at or above 6,000 feet above sea level.

CLEAR-ly A Winner.

Lake Tahoe is also one of the clearest lakes in the world. As of 2021, its average clarity is 73.1 feet from the surface. Lake Tahoe's water quality is 99.994% pure, rendering a glass of Tahoe water just shy of commercially distilled water (99.998% pure).

Ooh, Shine, Alpine!

Although it is considered an alpine "mountain" lake, Tahoe has no direct outlet to the sea. Instead, its water drains east of the Sierra Nevada by way of the Truckee River which flows 100 miles to evaporate in Pyramid Lake. This means, by definition, Lake Tahoe is a Great Basin "desert" lake.

Deepers, Creepers!

Lake Tahoe has an average depth of 997 feet and bottoms out at 1,645 feet. With these numbers, Lake Tahoe is the 2nd deepest lake in the USA, third deepest in North America, and 11th deepest in the world.

Deepening the Perspective

Let's wrap our heads around that.

Tahoe's depth is so insane that the elevation of Carson City is only 85 feet higher than the deepest part of Tahoe. Most alluring of all: if One World Trade Center (currently the tallest building in North America at 1,776 feet high) were to be dropped in the lake at its deepest point, only a bare 131 feet of the top of the building would be visible.

Now we're just showing off.

Lake Tahoe receives an average of—get ready for this—212 *billion* gallons of water every year: 65% of its water supply comes from its 63 tributaries and its 312-square mile watershed. The remaining 35% comes from rain and snow. Let's put this into perspective: there is enough water in Lake Tahoe that if it could be drained, would fill the entire state of California in one foot of water.

There. How'd that taste?

Largest Lakebed in North America

I bet when you think "Black Rock," you think "Burning Man" — the world-famous shindig that fosters about 100,000 people every year. The allure and secret sauce of Black Rock can go far beyond the idea of an annual pilgrimage, or a temporary week-long city.

When we use the name *"Black Rock,"* we could be discussing the whole of the area— a watershed that covers 11,600 square miles of the Great Basin! However, the feature that best defines the name "Black Rock" is the masterpiece itself, the Black Rock Playa: a massive and glistening Y-shaped salt pan that stretches for 102 miles from north to south.

Mystical Wonder

Geologically, the Black Rock playa functions as an outlet for the intermittent Quinn River and several small watercourses flowing in from three neighboring mountain ranges. During the winter, the playa magically transforms into a knee-deep inland sea – almost as if it was nostalgic for when it was a part of ancient Lake Lahontan some 10,000 years ago. When the playa remains wet for at least a month, the shallow waters then teem with fairy shrimp – tiny crustaceans that lay dormant in the salt crust, lying in wait for the lake's inevitable transformation.

Due to this unique semi-oasis factor, the Black Rock attracts more than 250 species of birds and waterfowl that stop in this arid country to rest and feed. Aside from the playa, the Black Rock Desert embraces dozens of natural hot springs and riparian pockets that showcase the amazing resources within this formidable landscape!

Since then, humans of modern year have realized the area's immense ecological value. In 2000, the Desert fell under protection of the (*inhale*) Black Rock Desert-High Rock Canyon Emigrant Trails National Conservation Area (NCA). The NCA placed some seventy percent of the lake playa under "Wilderness status" along with a unique mix of the natural hot springs, verdant canyons, and forested mountains once able to be reached by vehicle, now accessible only on foot.

Naturally, this has led to debate over public access, but en masse, presents a fantastic example of the integral conservation efforts of our desert lands.

Largest Wildlife Refuge in the Continental U.S.

Encompassing 1.65 million acres, the primary objective of the Desert NWR of southern Nevada is to protect the Desert Bighorn Sheep and its habitat. This huge refuge (the largest in the lower 48, in fact!) sort of sits off the radar, but its huge contribution to our state's wildlife and habitat resonates statewide.

Desert undergoes continual development of new water sources and improving upon existing ones so that Desert Bighorn can successfully rebound. It's estimated that 1,500 animals (more than any other place in the world) roam six mountain ranges and valleys protected within the sanctuary.

Don't let it's bleak appearance from the highway fool you! The Refuge encloses over forty natural springs, old-growth Joshua trees, rich conifer forests, and multiple groves of old-growth Bristlecone Pine atop the highest peaks. Visitors can sight see, photograph, camp, hike, or backpack in this very wild country that's all-too-often under-utilized.

> ○ DESERT NWR IS LOCATED JUST 30 MINUTES NORTH OF DOWNTOWN LAS VEGAS.
>
> Follow US 95 north to Corn Creek Road, then another 4 miles to the Corn Creek Visitor Center. You can easily spend days exploring this massive refuge by escaping into its rich Joshua tree communities, and even multi-day hikes into its surprising pine forests. Of course, take to the canyons for a decent chance of seeing our state animal with your own eyes.

Largest Hotel-Casino

There's no question that the MGM Grand in Las Vegas would be considered a palace in some other countries. This place is so grand that we need an entire list grand enough to hold its grandness. Holy Grand, that's a lot of grand.

The MGM Grand is the third largest hotel in the world and the largest hotel resort complex in the United States. The MGM was even the largest hotel in the world when it opened in 1993!

MGM takes up a full city block in between Harmon and Tropicana Avenues on the Las Vegas Strip. The complex is so massive it's actually linked by a series of overhead pedestrian bridges to four neighboring casinos.

The 30-floor main building stands 293 feet high, serving Las Vegas with approximately 6,852 rooms: *the most hotel rooms in a single complex in the United States.*

The property includes five outdoor pools, three rivers , and eight waterfalls that cover 6.6 acres as well as a 380,000 square foot convention center, the Grand Spa, CBS Television City (Studio 54), and MGM Grand Garden Arena.

The hotel showboats 13 live shows and night clubs, numerous shops (at last count 34), 19 restaurants as well as *the largest casino in Nevada which occupies a whopping 171,500 square feet.*

Nevada's Hidden Mansion

Did you know the MGM Grand also hosts one of the most expensive mansions in the world? The 100,000 square foot palace, known as the "King Suite," is strictly off-limits and out of view from the general public. To the average tourist, the King Suite will be completely un-noticeable and hidden behind a 20-foot concrete wall along the sidewalk of the Strip. So, save for a few videos of it on YouTube, you'll never get the chance of laying eyes on it...unless your wallet has no limits.

What do I get at the King Suite?

Not surprisingly, staying at this Romanesque mansion will generate quite a buzz. Here, you'll enjoy your very own 1,500 square foot swimming pool with private patio, exercise and conference rooms, a themed dance floor of your choice, a bowling alley, and a 2,000 square foot kitchen complete with your own 24-hour butler service.

Nope. That's not enough.

This package deal comes with your very own complimentary movie theater with a library of your choosing, and not one, not two, not three, but *four* complimentary Rolls-Royce's getting you to and from your favored destinations. You know, just in case one Rolls wasn't enough.

Grand enough for you? All of this can be yours for the low cost of $12,400 per night *and* by spending a minimum of $1 million inside the MGM Grand Casino.

Only in Vegas.

Largest Body of Water

The completion of a single dam formed an enormous blue-green body of water that has no equal. At 112 miles long and covering 247 square miles, Lake Mead is the largest reservoir in the United States.

The construction of Hoover (Boulder) Dam in April 1931 forever changed the wild and untamed nature of the Colorado River. Several billion tons of concrete formed a lake that boasts approximately 26,134,000 acre-feet of water, and at full pool—489 feet of water at its deepest point.

From above, this huge impound resembles a giant spider with hundreds of fingers, arms, and coves that rack up an impressive 550 miles of shoreline!

California, Nevada, and Arizona shares water rights to Lake Mead, and specifically the Colorado River, but it's Nevada that gets the short straw. Yet despite the enormous demand by the city of Las Vegas, she retains less than ten percent of the water rights.

Of the three states, California consumes the most water, using 72 percent for both urban use and agriculture.

Despite its size, Mead has succumbed to drought four times in the last fifty years—a poignant reminder of the ongoing challenge of water management in the West. Hydrologists and state officials from all three states have put forth new laws and smart practices regarding water usage on a river already tired and sucked dry.

Anything but *Mead*ian

The National Park Service manages Lake Mead (along with Lake Mohave) via the massive 1.5 million acre Lake Mead National Recreation Area (NRA). The NRA caters to over four million visitors a year, the fifth busiest national park in the system, all of whom who come to frolic in her fantastically warm winters, abundant water recreation, and the landscape's stunning red rock country.

My personal favorite, the park also preserves over seventy miles of the Colorado River in its most pristine state, much as it was before the formation of the reservoir. Here you can boat down river canyons and relax yourself beneath hot waterfalls, aqua blue water caves, and sprawl out on remote sandy beaches few people have seen. Sign me up!

Did you know?

Lake Mead is the only lake in Nevada with an outlet to the ocean... you know, if the Colorado River ever reaches the ocean!

That's right. By the time the Colorado reaches Mexico, the river has all been tapped dry and dies in a ghostly rivulet about forty miles north of its destination at the Gulf of California. Sadly, even in the wettest of years the Colorado River rarely, if ever, makes it to the sea.

Largest Hot Spring

Nevada has more hot springs than any other state in the country, yet few of them are as unexpected as the state's largest geothermal hot spring. Or, it this case should we say, boiling pond?

Diana's Punchbowl was named after the Roman goddess of springs and brooks, and like a goddess, Diana is on a scale all on her own.

Most hot springs in Nevada gurgle as small pools of lukewarm to boiling hot water innocently puncturing the desert floor, and yours to soak to your heart's content.

SILVER STATE SUPERLATIVES

At first glance, Diana isn't unlike a remote leviathan in the middle of the desert; she spews steam, churns with roasting water, and roars with geothermal gases.

When you come at her from any direction all you're met with is a rather staid, white chalky hill surrounded by miles of open space—giving you no impression that you're about to stumble onto a broiling 600-foot high, sheer-sided travertine bowl. After parking and walking a short distance, you find yourself a bit unnerved, standing on top of Hell's well and staring down into the abyss.

The bowl, more like the belly of the beast, measures about fifty feet across with nearly sheer vertical walls that drop down about thirty feet to a pool of 200-degree water that only my wife is crazy enough to want to soak in.

Oddly, the BLM has not installed a fence around the hole to keep two-legged morons from falling to their deaths. That means a single misstep leaves the imagination to shiver. Standing at the lip of the bowl you can't help but be taken away by the spring's blue-green waters.

This is one hot spring that you cannot indulge, yet it's one marvel that will surely take your breath away.

> FIND DIANA'S PUNCHBOWL IN THE MIDDLE OF MONITOR VALLEY IN CENTRAL NEVADA. From Austin, head east on US 50 for about 26 miles to the unpaved Monitor Valley Road. Look for a large green sign pointing to "Belmont, Manhattan." Follow this gravel highway for 35 miles to Diana's doorstep. Just look for the only big white hill in the middle of nowhere. The BLM has opted to keep this place as untainted as possible. If you choose to visit, please be a good human and leave only footprints.

Largest State Park

Located just one hour north of Las Vegas, Valley of Fire is NEVADA'S FIRST AND LARGEST STATE PARK.

Valley of Fire is our state's version of the red canyon country of the American Southwest, and oozing at the seams with its unusual, fiery red sandstone formations. This is a place bulging with petroglyph fields, red rock spires, fins, hoodoos, arches, sandstone vistas, and colorful slot canyons.

Valley began as a generous 8,500 acre parcel given by the Federal Government in 1925 and was officially established by the state in 1935. According to the state park system, the park receives an average of 500,000 visitors per year—second only to Lake Tahoe-Nevada State Park.

The park has since become a paradise, a muse for artists who come from around the world.

We'll let the names alone inspire you: Elephant Rock, Arch Rock, and Atlatl Rock (which is adorned by native petroglyphs); Mouse's Tank; Windstone Arch; the Seven Sisters; the Fire Wave; White Domes; Fire Canyon; and the park's highlight, Rainbow Vista.

Largest Silver Strike in U.S. History

Nevada's mining legacy is legendary, and no other spot on the map showcases what could perhaps be the most coveted of Battle Born's superlatives. "Queen of the Comstock." "The Hill." "The Lode" (as it soon came to be called), or as you know it, Virginia City, would eventually become the largest silver strike ever to occur on American soil.

The year was 1857. The setting — a wild, undiscovered region off the world map.

"The Lode" was secretly discovered by Hosiah and Allen Grosch, then "rediscovered" again in January of 1859 by James "Old Virginny" Fennimore. Upon Fennimore's "discovery," several prospectors questioned the validity of the old drunk, namely an outspoken fellow by the name of Henry Comstock. At the risk of word spreading, he went into business with Finney by promising to share the wealth.

The men worked at the earth for months but were quickly losing patience with the obnoxious quagmires of sticky "blue mud" that clung to their spades and axes, overall preventing them from getting very far.

The rock itself and the ore they broke their backs to work had assayed hardly anything. In a sick twist of fate, it turns out the blue muck that caused them so much grief was the secret bearer of riches, worth an unbelievable value of $5,000 a ton.

The Rush to Washoe

By the spring of 1860, the "Rush to Washoe" was on--with hopefuls arriving by the thousands. "Gold Hill," "Silver City," and the "Queen of the Comstock" (later named Virginia City), earned their place on maps, first across the nation, then on maps across the world.

Within a few months, mining companies from all over the globe took over individual mining claims, creating steady jobs for every healthy man who could work. The Silver Queen certainly became the largest city in this previously unpopulated territory.

Visit today and it's easy to imagine all of this amazing energy taking center stage.

Today, Virginia City bursts at the seams with flamboyant parades, mock shootouts, and bawdy souvenir shops, but in her roots, Virginia City was indeed, as quoted by the *Territorial Enterprise,* the "Richest Place on Earth."

Ponder this!

The growth of San Francisco itself is largely due to the Comstock Lode. The city's shipping docks, assay offices, and financial enterprises—including three of its five super banks—were owned and paid for by Virginia City stock.

In 1864, Comstock silver funded the last months of the Civil War ultimately begging the question: did Virginia City lead the Union to victory?

And finally, Virginia City might be why Nevada is its own state and not just a part of Utah or California. In 1864, President Lincoln admitted Nevada into the Union as the 36th state for none other than its silver.

The reverberating effect of the Comstock Lode across the nation was nothing short of amazing. Despite the rapid growth and identity crisis of western Nevada today, Virginia City retains its rustic charm. Even amidst the fluff of touristy stuff, the whiff of historical dominance solidly remains in the air.

When you drive up and around Greiner's Bend on 342 there's no ignoring the gigantic gash on the mountain's back: aka, the stark reminder of the great mining legacy that led to our statehood.

Smallest Border Town

© Tad Hetu

The definition of a *border town* is any community that straddles the Nevada state line, predominantly to serve gaming and alcohol to nearby residents of a neighboring state.

The idea is so engrained in her roots, that Nevada is defined by her border communities.

From the largest border town of Boulder City (with a population of 14,879 as of 2021) we travel seven hundred miles to the north to find ourselves in THE SMALLEST AND MOST REMOTE BORDER COMMUNITY IN NEVADA.

With less than twenty year-round residents (2021), the tiny outpost of Denio (pronounced di-NYE-oh) sits on one of the most isolated sections of the Oregon/Nevada state line with the nearest population center over 100 miles away in any direction. This place is so remote, it has no open year-round establishments.

SILVER STATE SUPERLATIVES

Instead, residents handed over the *Everything-Nevada* fix to Denio Junction. This single service station, just two miles away, offers cheap gasoline and conveniences, the needed slot room, and a full bar and restaurant in order to serve any off-beaten travelers in this neck of the woods.

Here's the catch: Denio Junction is not a fully registered town and being two miles south of the state line, is it thereby disqualified as a full-fledged border town?

As such, how do we rate this one? Can we be a little looser in our definition of a border town?

We don't *Denio* it. It's an interesting case—more like a reclusive renegade that must be found to be appreciated. Being so far away from well... everything, one can't just stumble into Denio, but for your sake, let's hope you do!

Residents here will swear they are surrounded by some of the wildest country anywhere in the West.

> FOLLOW SR 292 NORTH FROM SR 140 to find this little bubble of community out here in the middle of nowhere. SR 292 ends at the state line, but you can follow the paved Fields-Denio Road north to Fields and the rest of the Beaver State on Oregon Highway 205. You'll find yourself enveloped in the quiet starkness of southeast Oregon while you attempt to get back to civilization. Prepare for a long 2.5 hour drive back on SR 140 to Winnemucca or 1 hour to Adel, about an hour east of Lakeview.

Smallest State Park

This tiny slice of Nevada's state park system doesn't receive nearly the praise and press as the other four nearby parks in the area. The bite-sized Elgin Schoolhouse is proof that size doesn't matter, and at less than an acre in size, it takes the crown as THE STATE'S SMALLEST STATE PARK.

Nestled in the unbelievably beautiful Rainbow Canyon just twenty minutes south of Caliente, what you're getting here is a one-room schoolhouse that served several generations of students from grades 1-8 from 1922 to 1967.

In 1924, the addition of a teachers' apartment solved all of the staffing issues in this relatively isolated area of the state.

Aside from the amazing preservation of the building itself, many of the school's furnishings are original to the era and on display inside the schoolhouse. The main classroom beams to life with student and teacher's desks, a wood burning stove, and a vintage piano, backdropped by the chalkboard's daily lesson displayed. You'll also have access to the teacher's private apartment affixed to the back of the schoolhouse complete with a kitchen and bedroom with identical period-specific artifacts of early Rainbow Canyon residents.

While nearby Kershaw-Ryan and Cathedral Gorge State Parks may blow you away with their incredible unearthly landscapes, there's something uniquely magical about stepping back in time at this tiniest of state parks.

> From Caliente, drive south on SR 317 past Kershaw-Ryan State Park for 21 miles through scenic Rainbow Canyon and watch for a brown sign into the tiny town of Elgin. Cross the railroad tracks and park anywhere outside the gate. The park boundary begins at the fence line along the tracks. Tours of the Schoolhouse are arranged by appointment only. As there is no official office for this tiny park, please call Kershaw-Ryan State Park to schedule an appointment at 775-726-3564.

Smallest Community

We searched all over the Nevada map for the one to take this mini tiara and, well ... instead of a drumroll, enter the winning contestant with a booming kazoo.

Think of roads in the middle of oblivion that veer off the main highway and jettison straight out to a pinpoint on the horizon. This classic scene in Nevada is best personified by the former mining camp of Gold Point, er ... that mere blip on the horizon.

In a state chock full of tiny smatterings of population crowning this old bird was no easy task as Gold Point had plenty of runners-up waiting to nab the reward of THE SMALLEST BONAFIDE TOWN IN NEVADA.

Horn A-What?

Formerly known as Lime Point, then Hornsilver, the name Gold Point officially stuck when high-grade ore was discovered here in 1908. Major mining efforts ceased during World War II, but since then, somehow residents have always been drawn back to this place smack dab in the middle of nowhere.

Gold Point is the only form of reference in this desolate part of the Silver State roughly in between Goldfield and Beatty. This place is so lost that the county sheriff rolls through just once a month. It's the kind of place where the locals (all eight of them) swear the ghosts of prospectors past sometimes let out eerie heehaws in the dead of night.

Gold Point may not exist today if it weren't for Las Vegas native Herb Robbins, who with partner Walt Kremin, owns most of the town's buildings. They came across Gold Point in the late 70s and while only a few hardy residents remained at the time, dozens of buildings stood rotting under the desert sun along the town's main street. When the opportunity arose, both Herb and his friend Chuck purchased the Post Office and General Store which came complete with original furnishings. During weekends, Herb assumes the role as Sheriff and fire chief.

To this day, all mail is delivered to Goldfield. All forms of food must be brought in from neighboring communities, the largest being Beatty, 67 miles away. Before the arrival of cellphones, the nearest public call box was 20 miles away at the defunct Cotton Tail brothel.

Needless to say, Gold Point eats isolation for breakfast.

Be sure to pony up and take a trip back in time inside the Gold Point Bed and Breakfast. Ask to *"see the saloon"* and you'll be courted inside to fancy a picture-perfect old west scene and a virtual step back in time. While you're out here, you can stay in an original, historic miners' cabin under one of the cleanest, darkest skies in America.

EPIC & AWESOME

These superlatives couldn't fit into any of the previous categories, yet they're among our favorites. These fine facts best represent Nevada in all of its gnarly glory.

Most Expensive Hotel Room in the World

IN A STATE KNOWN for its budget stays and cheap hotel rooms, Nevada crunches irony by equally hosting to a fair share of overindulgent stays that most of us will only view in photographs. If you ever find yourself at the Palms Resort & Casino in Las Vegas with a small fortune, consider indulging a night's stay in not only Nevada's priciest room, but THE MOST EXPENSIVE HOTEL ROOM IN THE WORLD.

Here's what you do:

Amble on up to the front desk of the Palms Resort and ask about the Empathy Suite. Stand back and observe the reaction of the desk clerk. Suddenly, regular talk will shift to whispered tones. Walkie-talkies emerge from nowhere. The manager and his/her minions appear in a cloud of smoke with dollar signs in their eyes.

It's then you know you've stumbled onto something larger than life.

Oh, and just to avoid looky-loos and to prove your seriousness, reservations need to be requested first before confirming any official bookings. The Palms website doesn't even list the suite for the bourgeoisie to salivate over. At an eye-watering $100k per night (and a two-night minimum), the world's most expensive hotel room isn't just a fantasy.

Located on the 34th & 35th floors of the hotel, the two-story Empathy Suite was designed by renowned British artist Damien Hirst. It features several of his more famous works—the most famous piece showcasing two real (but not live) Bull Sharks suspended in formaldehyde.

A view of the mystical Empathy Suite from my 18th-floor hotel room across the street. And yes. I booked a room just to get this shot. 2022.

At 9,000 square feet, you'll receive an eighteen-seat bar top along with the main sitting room (out of five) which can accommodate over fifty people, The second floor tops you off with two master bedrooms, a rotating bed, massage rooms, a salt relaxation room, your own personal gym, a powder room, and an eight person Jacuzzi.

Oh, and let's not forget the over-hanging balcony pool 34 floors above the Strip!

Upon arrival, you'll get 24-hour butler and chauffeured car services, a private art tour of the hotel, and just to sweeten your already gold enlaced taste buds—a $10,000 credit to use at the hotel. Generally, the Empathy is provided at no charge to *The Whales*, a term given to players with a minimum $1 million line of credit in the casino.

We're not done. Why not accompany this ridiculously priced accommodation here with our next two superlatives?

Most Expensive Cocktail

Given that we have the most lenient liquor laws in the entire country, it's only fitting that we go all out with the stuff here in the Silver State. Ounce for ounce, we discovered THE MOST EXPENSIVE MIXED DRINK IN THE STATE behind the closed doors of a Vegas nightclub. Are you surprised?

If you have no restrictions on the greenbacks, find the XS Nightclub inside the Wynn and ask for *The Ono*. This royal libation has no feigns about over-the-top luxury if you happen to be stashing approximately ten thousand bucks in your back pocket.

Don't worry. We know what you're thinking. Let's see what goes into a five-digit cocktail shall we?

One coming right up!

The Ono features a rare cognac that alone inspired the cocktail: the luscious, Remy Martin Louis XVIII Black Pearl that by itself retails for over $2,000 per shot. Next, comes an addition of the Charles Heidsieck 1981 Champagne Charlie, a vintage treasure that goes for over $500 per bottle. Ultimately, it's because of this wine that *The Ono* will only exist for a short period.

The Charles Heidsieck company stopped making vintages of Champagne Charlie in 1985; thus, once the vintage is gone, it's *gone forever*. So, why not get one while you can, you know, if you can afford to do so without getting a second mortgage on your home.

Surprisingly, the Ono wasn't conjured to simply make money. This, my friends, is a full-blown experience. The drink was carefully curated and celebrates the flavor and scarcity of both the cognac and the champagne, served delicately to patrons in custom-designed glassware.

Second Best is Cool Too!

Are you a few thousand bucks short? Perfect, because you can swing over to the Tryst nightclub inside the MGM Grand and ask for the *Menage à Trois*—by our research, the second runner-up to the Ono.

This sinful concoction of Cristal Rosé, Hennessy Ellipse, and Grand Mernier Cent-Cinquantenaire is decorated with 23-karat gold flakes and liquid gold syrup. It also includes a gold straw, studded with a nine-point diamond-yours for a grand total of $3,000 a glass.

At least you can keep the straw.

Most Expensive Restaurant

Once you've got that ostentatious Empathy Suite booked, and you've ordered your precious Ono, it's time for some dinner. Take a mosey down the Strip to Caesar's Palace where you'll find the most expensive restaurant in the Silver State. I mean, seriously. When did you last indulge yourself so thoroughly?

When you enter the main casino at Caesar's Palace, make your way to Augustus Tower and look for the name Guy Savoy emblazoned above the two giant wooden doors. Guy is one of the best chefs in France with numerous accolades for haute cuisine *à son nom* (under his name) most notably two coveted Michelin Stars.

He's also mentored other world class chefs, including Thomas Keller and Gordon Ramsay. *Simplement*, along with executive Julien Asseo, his attention to detail creates nothing but an unforgettable dining experience.

Très bien! Des prix?

But, of course. The cost. What makes this the most expensive restaurant in Nevada? *Restaurant Guy Savoy* is nothing less than an indulgence of taste and an immersion of elegant French cuisine. You don't simply visit the restaurant. You come with the expectation of being fully immersed in an elegant, authentic setting that's almost as good as the food.

Associate Jean-Michel Wilmotte designed the dining room as a near replica of the original restaurant in Paris. The Las Vegas menu intentionally mirrors its Paris sister restaurant with what it serves for the season: so authentic that it's easy to forget you're in the middle of the American desert.

Even though his name is synonymous with the restaurant, Executive Chef Julien Asseo ensures every dish at Guy Savoy is a meticulously crafted canvas of exquisite taste and presentation. Here's how it works.

Food choices are based on the restaurant's two menus: *Guy Savoy's Signature* menu is $290 per person. An optional wine pairing will tack on an additional $175 per person, with a premium wine pairing at $375.

The *Innovation Inspiration* Menu is $375 per person, with the optional wine pairing of $200 and the premium wine pairing at $375. Oh, and since there's a two-person minimum reservation, expect to hand over at least a thousand bucks for a night. However, it isn't all that uncommon to see Guy Savoy himself touching tables, coming out to ensure a flawless experience.

Care to Krug?

The highlight, and the talk of Las Vegas in fact, is the pinnacle of indulgence: a 9-course dinner at the Krug table. Reservations are mandatory here at the only Krug Room in the United States. You'll be walked through the multi-course extravaganza by the chef himself as it comes straight from the line to your table.

Over all nine courses, the chef prides himself on delivering a symphony of flavors delicately crafted for this exclusive experience. Every meal is unique and the total experience (and cost) will be based on what you order. It isn't uncommon to fork over a cool 3Gs on this dining affair.

Finally, regardless of your menu choice, les sommeliers will ask you about an optional wine pairing for your meals to add a personalized touch to your dining experience from the restaurant's *Wine Sanctuary*. This 2,000 square foot cave boasts an extraordinary selection of over 12,000 bottles.

These range from "simple" $300 bottles, to historical vintages spanning over a century, and even exclusive wines from world-renowned producers that remain under lock and key.

Among the many menu options, you'll find such treasures as the "Colors of Caviar," the world-famous Artichoke Truffle Soup, Iceberg Salmon, the Open Mille-Feuille, Roasted Guinea Fowl, and about 25 other options to completely break your bank account.

> *Restaurant Guy Savoy* is open for dinner from 5:30 until 9:30 p.m. Wednesday through Sunday. It is closed on Monday and Tuesday. Despite the restaurant's high-end appeal, business casual dress is sufficient, but semi-formal attire is generally expected. In typical French fashion, plan on a leisurely evening, as meals are meant to be savored. You'll want to allow at least three hours for a meal at the most expensive restaurant in Nevada.

The Paiute Princess

Sarah Winnemucca—daughter of Chief Winnemucca, and granddaughter of Captain Truckee—has perhaps no other influential equal in American history. She's right up there with the greats: John Muir, Rosa Parks, Paul McCartney... And best yet, she came from right here in the Silver State.

Miss Winnemucca's contributions to the very rights of individuals still resonates loudly today and we as Nevadans celebrate her with a few incredible superlatives to her name.

Born in 1844 near the Humboldt River Sink, Sarah Winnemucca came from a legendary family of Paiute leaders. Even from her birth, she was a steady presence when the Paiutes' homeland and way of life were ostensibly threatened by the influx of white settlers.

From an early age, her grandfather insisted she be well educated. During a period in the 1850's, she learned the ways of the white world to better understand the new working societies around her; she mastered the English language that would one day enable her to bring the Paiute cause to the forefront of the nation.

Sarah had mastered English so well that she became an interpreter for the U.S. Army at Camp McDermitt in 1869 and later an assistant teacher at Malheur Reservation in Oregon.

Her fluencies in English, Spanish, and a handful of Native American languages even earned her the reputation as a trusted associate of many prominent figures.

When the Bannock War broke out in 1878, she served the army as a scout, messenger, interpreter, and close associate of commanding General Oliver Howard.

Simultaneously and in secret, she led her father's band to safety from the enemy camp. Her bravery in the face of danger and her epic long-distance rides over harsh terrain are the stuff of western legend.

The War of Words

After the war, all the Paiutes who had deserted Malheur Reservation were forced into exile at the Yakima Reservation, regardless of whether they had participated in the war or not. This was a cruel and unjust punishment, violating commitments made by the government to the Paiutes.

Because of their displacement, so many people perished from the diseases prevalent at Yakima that they overflowed the graveyard, and the reservation agent ordered their bodies thrown into the Columbia River.

It was then that Sarah made every effort to get her people back to their native homeland in Nevada.

She lectured in San Francisco on their plight to arouse public opinion. She traveled to Washington, D.C. with her father, brother and one of the Paiute headmen to appeal to Secretary of the Interior Carl Schurz to win their release. With Schurz's written promise that the Paiutes "might" return home, Winnemucca made another one of her epic rides through snow and danger to bring the message to Yakima, only for Schurz to change his mind.

Bitter and forlorn, she would later write that his *"promises which, like the wind, were heard no more."*

Soon she was evicted from the reservations, but Sarah counseled her people from remote locations to undertake a program of passive resistance.

"Refuse to farm," she told them.

"Build no houses, do nothing to indicate that you will accept staying at Yakama [sic]."

Over time, the Paiutes escaped the reservation in small groups. In 1883, she conducted a lecture tour of the east coast before receiving help from sympathetic supporters in the West. Sarah's plight had broken ground with the debut of a book about her people's treatment, entitled *Life among the Piutes: Their wrongs and claims*.

Drumroll, Please!

With the release of her works, Sarah Winnemucca became THE FIRST NATIVE AMERICAN WOMAN TO SECURE A COPYRIGHT AND TO PUBLISH IN THE ENGLISH LANGUAGE, which of course, is impressive enough as is. In addition, her book was THE FIRST BOOK EVER WRITTEN BY A NATIVE AMERICAN.

Unfortunately, Sarah's activity only infuriated the Indian agents more and rebirthed a hatred for her and the native Paiutes. People went so far as denouncing her "a common prostitute" and defiling her name with accusations of her being addicted to drunkenness and gambling.

She responded with only commendations from prominent military figures and political leaders familiar with her efforts and, like a 19th century mic drop, included her harassers in her book.

She is most famous for the series of lectures she would give for her people later in life until she passed away in 1891. The remarkable Paiute Princess would dress in ceremonial outfit and speak of the injustices experienced by Native Americans using her charisma and magnetic personality.

Sarah Winnemucca was inducted into the Nevada Writers Hall of Fame in 1993.

Sarah Winnemucca, 1844-1891.

Today, she is honored by a six-foot tall marble statue, which was ceremoniously constructed here in Nevada and gifted to the United States Capitol in Washington D.C. The statue now sits in the center of Emancipation Hall depicting Sarah as she looked when she was 35 years old with waist-long hair in full Paiute costume ... and in Sarah's character, her book full of heartfelt efforts clenched tightly in her right hand.

Deadliest Mining Camp

Do yourself a favor. If you dare.

Head fifty-five miles south of Pioche, half of which will be on a dusty washboard road, and you'll find yourself at one of our favorite superlatives: the miserable mining camp of Delamar, THE DEADLIEST MINING CAMP IN OUR STATE'S HISTORY.

Most people might conclude this title with big brother Pioche to the north, but unlike Pioche where numerous residents met their end spaghetti-western style so often romanticized in films, Delamar's death maker was much more methodical. In fact, Delamar was so bad, its reputation spread across the state. This was truly a nightmare zone you'd hope not to find yourself.

The Devil's Profits

The discovery of very rich gold ore in 1889 prompted a wave of prospectors into this very remote patch in the Mojave Desert. In fact, Delamar's setting is so isolated that all materials at the time had to be brought by mule-team through the mountains 150 miles from a railroad yard in Utah.

To make things worse, Delamar had no form of water whatsoever. Rain and snow were rare commodities. No underground springs. No options. Every ounce of the precious liquid came from Meadow Valley Wash, 12 miles away.

Every drop, rationed, tainted, monopolized, or all three.

Delamar was so parched, all processes to mill the ore had to be done by dry milling, or crushing of the ore. This dry milling created a fine, toxic silica or "death dust" that buried itself deep in the lungs of not only the thousands of miners underground, but virtually anybody nearby. With this silent terror ever lingering, Delamar had more cases of Silicosis (Miner's Cough) than any other camp in Nevada.

As such, the town received the nickname "The Widowmaker" from the thousands of prematurely dead due to this disease. While exact numbers are enigmatic (even with my insane hours of research), historians estimate that at least one out of ten miners came down with Silicosis and with it, an almost certain death. Legend says that there were over 400 widows living in Delamar at one time. The nickname didn't last long, as the brutal, dry conditions proved too much for the people living there. The last resident left this miserable place in the spring of 1900.

Delamar was one of the state's leading gold producers of all time - topping out at a whopping $15 million produced in its lonely, desolate lifetime. Truly, a sick irony.

> THOUGH AN UNIMAGINABLY TERRIBLE PLACE TO LIVE IN YESTERYEAR, THE RUINS AT DELAMAR ARE SOME OF THE MOST INTERESTING IN NEVADA TODAY. Do yourself a favor and pack plenty of water and head south out of Caliente on US 93 for 42.8 miles to the historical marker atop Hancock Pass. Stop and read the historical marker for Delamar and head south on this dusty, graded road for 12.3 miles to the town site. Though it's only a short distance, the incredibly rough washboard will definitely slow you down, so prepare yourself for about a 45-minute ride to the town from here.

Tallest Structure

Not counting our lavish hotel-casinos, Nevada isn't a state synonymous with tall or towering structures—until you remember the mighty Stratosphere Tower punching the Las Vegas sky.

At 1,150 feet, the Strat is not only the tallest structure in the Silver State, but also holds tight as the tallest observation tower in the United States, and THE TALLEST STRUCTURE WEST OF THE MISSISSIPPI RIVER.

The Stratosphere Tower was built in 1996 as the centerpiece for the new half-dozen casino-hotels surrounding Sahara Avenue. The opening of the Strat charmed numerous financial opportunities that arose to soak in its glory.

Most noteworthy is the flurry of thrill-seekers that followed.

Enjoy the SkyPod is a mesmerizing experience on its own that takes you to the very top of the tower, with exquisite dining and drinks to help you soak in the best view in all the city.

 You can also take in one of the three thrill rides at the very top of the structure that fill up fast during the summer. *Insanity*, *X Scream*, and *Big Shot* power through with 5Gs of force and teasing teeter-totters over a thousand feet above the Las Vegas Valley.

If you'd like a little more action than just riding things out, why not bungee jump off the damn thing? Acrophobiacs need not apply.

Yup, this superlative surprised us too. Seattle's Space Needle and LA's piddly towers of concrete have nothing on us.

Tallest Waterfall

As the driest state in the country, it's hard to imagine Nevada with natural waterfalls. In fact, most waterfall maps and websites ignore our state completely, yet Nevada hides many gems that will take your breath away.

Instead of rushing whitewater and the intense spray monsters of the Pacific Northwest, the hidden waterfalls of Nevada steal the show in their unexpectedness.

This one absolutely blew our minds across the desert floor.

The hidden oasis of Stonewall Falls is one you're not likely to hear about. Driving the barren lands on US 95, the last thing you would expect to find is a waterfall. But there it is, a giant gash cut into a single mountain within the government-owned Nellis Air Force Range just outside of Goldfield.

Stonewall Falls itself is rarely more than a trickle, but in this particularly arid region, this little dribble of water is a priceless lifeblood. This amazing gem is fed by year-round Stonewall Spring and uniquely stair steps 401 feet into a tiny pool met by a small patch of moss and wildflowers: the flows certainly diminutive, but miraculous.

Scientists on the air base have monitored the spring flow over the past five decades and, sadly, Stonewall may not be around in the next five decades. Get out there and have your breath taken away by NEVADA'S TALLEST WATERFALL before it's too late.

📍 Getting to the state's tallest waterfall

First, we ask that you follow these directions VERY carefully as remote rural nevada conditions change constantly. Please do your homework before you embark. For the preservation of this sensitive oasis and per the request of Nellis Air Force Range, we have omitted all GPS coordinates to Stonewall Falls. Please do not call the base to request GPS! They will not give it out because of security reasons. Capiche?

Trip your odometer as you leave Goldfield on US 95 and look to the left for an unmarked, graded road 14.4 miles south of town. Reset your odometer as you turn here and don't forget to close the road gate behind you. Follow this road for 2.9 miles to a fork. Turn right. Follow this new graded road to the east. Here, look for yet another road going off to the right. (This will be approximately 3.9 miles in from US 95.) It's here where you'll leave the graded road behind and continue east on this final dirt track. CONGRATULATIONS. YOU'RE HALFWAY THERE.

In about one-half mile, you will reach the perimeter fence and one of the few spots with public access onto the restricted Nellis Air Force Range. Here, you'll see a sign poignantly stating that you must remain on the road to avoid trespassing on the test range. Cameras abound so do not test it. Pass through the gate (closing it behind you) and continue toward the giant gash in the lone mountain on the horizon. This giant defile is the tallest waterfall in Nevada. Stay as long as you like during the day, but you must be off the Range by sunset. Considering the rare access to this amazing find, I think that's an incredible compromise that we should follow religiously.

His Excellency of the Only Micronation in Nevada © Grace Sebesta

Nevada's Only Micronation

Let's see. We've covered the highest point. The tallest waterfall. The most expensive cocktail. The highest alpine lake in the world. The oldest community. Well, points for effort on the community.

What about a random independently sovereign nation in the middle of a residential Northern Nevada neighborhood?

Created in 1977, the Republic of Molossia is a reputedly tiny enclave within Nevada completely surrounded by the United

States. Molossia has its own flag, currency, holidays, measurement system, national symbols, Railroad, Postal Service, and even its own Navy, Space Program, National Parks and time zone. While the country has its own constitution and national assembly, Molossia claims to be under "martial law" due to the "ever present threat" of the United States.

If you're looking to get out of the USA for a little while take a trip to Dayton, a town normally associated for its debate with Genoa for Nevada's oldest community. After fifteen minutes of zigzagging through residential Dayton you'll arrive at the customs station, known as the "Harmony Province" of Molossia. At just 0.020 acres, this happens to be the smallest province of the country as well as the capitol, Baughston.

Other provinces include *Neptune Deep* (the floor of the deepest trench in the Pacific Ocean) and Vesperia (about 50,000 square miles on the Planet Venus), both of which Molossia has appropriated.

The Tiniest Nation on Earth

To greet you into this sovereign nation is Molossia's founder and president, Kevin Baugh and his wife Adrianne—*ahem*, we mean *His Excellency President Baugh* and *Madame Adrienne*. On our visit, she was quite elated when my wife addressed her as *Her Excellency Ms. Adrienne, Keeper of the Pooch.*

This duo welcomes visitors by appointment only (walk-ins, aka foreign trespassers, will be permanently expelled from the nation) before being led on a guided tour of the country and its general infrastructure.

While passports are not necessary, they will be given an official stamp if presented. Most important to note is to leave your incandescent bulbs, catfish, walruses, onions, and anything from Texas in the car. These items are considered contraband and grounds for immediate permanent expulsion from the country.

Additionally, Kevin Baugh continues to pay property taxes on the land to secure "foreign aid" in the help to fight the ongoing war with East Germany. In an interview with *Atlas Obscura*, Baugh commented on the red tape of owning "foreign soil" – with it "being necessary for the future of the Molossian capitol." (Because you know running a country from the surface of Venus is a little difficult.)

> "We all want to think we have our own country, but you know the U.S. is a lot bigger."

Molossia's currency is the *valora*, which is subdivided into 100 *futtrus* and pegged to the relative value of Pillsbury cookie dough. Cookie dough is stored in an outbuilding called the Bank of Molossia from which *valora* coins (made from local casino chips) and printed banknotes are sold.

Still not convinced of Molossia's sovereignty? CNN's Big Story also featured Molossia and President Baugh with an "exclusive global tour" of the capitol.

Forget Rome or Greece this year. Book your 45-minute vacation for the ages to Molossia today!

📍 THE MICRONATION OF MOLOSSIA IS ON THE NORTHERN OUTSKIRTS OF DAYTON WITHIN THE RESIDENTIAL NEIGHBORHOOD OF SIX MILE CANYON. Molossia is so cool, even Google Maps clearly lists the coordinates as **39.322924, -119.539599 ("Republic of Molossia")**. From downtown Dayton, follow US 50 for 6.3 miles to La Fond Avenue. Take La Fond for 1.8 miles to Territory Road and turn left. Follow this for 0.6 miles and turn left onto Mary Lane where you'll find Kevin Baugh's property, Capitol of Harmony Province and the smallest micronation in the world. Please respect His Excellency's request to visit by appointment only. Though an independent nation, Baugh still calls Storey County Sheriffs to help with his foreign aid in expelling trespassers.

Book your free tour of Molossia at www.molossia.org.

The Geographical Center of Nevada

How would you like being the center of attention? Well, not that anybody would notice out here in the middle of Nevada. Literally.

During one of many research trips around the state, we decided to revel in the spotlight and concentrated our efforts to be that center of attention. Bagging the State Historical Markers of Lander and Eureka Counties allowed for this quick diversion off of "America's Loneliest Road" in search of the exact geographic center of Nevada. The following of wanderlust-driven people who have left their tally at "the Center" was proof enough we weren't the only ones fascinated with this geographic anomaly.

The center, although somewhat remote, isn't overly difficult to reach and doesn't demand a sturdy rig except after a thunderstorm or during the muddy season. It does, however, require a whimsical fit of curiosity.

Most references will disappoint you as simply referring to the Center at a spot *"26 miles southeast of Austin."* The U.S. Geological Society (USGS), however, has seen fit to record its location with the following GPS coordinates:

W116 37' 56.0, N39 19' 48.0

In 2009, we arrived at...a single rebar pole stuck into the earth. Next to it, a small flag marked this truly lonely patch of ground officially designated as THE GEOGRAPHIC CENTER OF NEVADA.

For the Silver State, we found it only fitting that this holy spot is in the middle of nowhere.

Keep in mind that our journey required us to weed through a dozen unique GPS coordinates listed by several sources. We conquered it long before the Center had made the touristy headlines of state publications, so you can be glad that you now have the luxury of merely taking my word for it!

So then, how do you define the precise geographical center in an irregularly wedge-shaped state like Nevada?

Fortunately, Nevada's shape isn't as complex as other states. I mean, how do we pinpoint the geographic center of say, Hawaii? The precise definition of a geographic center is something usually people can and will debate, so long as plenty research exists from different sources.

Here's a better idea. Just accept this little patch of earth into your open arms as the Geographic Center of our great state. In recent years, visitors have lovingly mounted a state flag here with a small coffee can to collect quarters (only Nevada quarters in honor of our mistress Battle Born). Soak in the stillness and let the sweet nothing and complete surrounding silence take your breath away, just as it did us years ago.

It might be the middle of nowhere, but we wouldn't have it any other way. It still felt like home.

> Thanks to a wide number of press out here in recent years, the state of Nevada has posted a sign and mounted a state flag to mark the Geographic Center of Nevada.

Start by getting to the tiny community of Austin, roughly 3 hours east of Reno. From Austin, continue east on US 50 for 26 miles over Hickison Summit to a large green sign to "Belmont." (If you've been paying attention, you'll see this is the same road for Diana's Punchbowl. Two-for-one deal, anyone?) Over the years, Google Maps has recognized the site based on the coordinates listed above, but don't be surprised if you don't get service out here. Do yourself a favor. Make it a routine to carry along the "black" (Benchmark) Nevada atlas and find it clearly listed as the "Center of Nevada."

Turn south here onto Belmont Road and follow this for approximately 14.5 miles to the set of coordinates listed above for Nevada's Geographic Center. (This will be the junction with Forest Road 004 to Wallace Canyon.)

Nevada's Only Port City

Anybody who's anybody knows that Nevada is a strictly landlocked state, proven by its immense deserts and snow-capped mountain ranges.

No way could there be a time and place when old Battle Born was connected to the sea. Right?

Wrong. Enter Callville, NEVADA'S ONLY PORT CITY. *Wait, what?*

A Call to Action

In the late 1850s, Mormon leader Brigham Young conjured a clear vision along the rock walls of the Colorado River: he wanted the ability for European immigrants to reach Utah from Panama, via passage up the river to a port city here in the Mojave Desert.

Never before had anybody thought up the idea of connecting this dry region to the ocean. Then on November 1, 1864, Young directed Anson Call to:

"Take a suitable company, locate a road to the Colorado, explore the river, find a suitable place for a warehouse, build it, and form a settlement at or near the landing."

To accomplish this, Call employed three men in St. George with explicit instructions to go *"one mile below the mouth of the narrows of Boulder Canyon and above the mouth of Black Canyon."* Here above the high water mark they located a black and rocky point which was considered a suitable spot for the warehouse, located just below the confluence of Callville Wash with the Colorado River.

Callville was officially established on the west bank of the river on December 2, 1864. During the Civil War, Callville acted double as an Army garrison and landing point for Colorado River steamboats from the Gulf of Mexico. Its run, however, was terminated when Octavius Decatur Gass (the local postmaster) surveyed the land and deemed it to be too far up the river for extended steamboat navigation.

One man's word was all it took.

By June of 1869 the port of Callville was abandoned, but the storehouse stood as late as 1892. Those looking to find this nifty superlative will need to bring some scuba gear. The site of Callville lies submerged under 400 feet beneath the waters of Lake Mead, all but concealing the old girl from the world.

Callville Bay retains the name and memory of Nevada's only port city to the ocean.

> THE SITE OF CALLVILLE CAN BE FOUND NEAR THE POSH COMMUNITY OF CALLVILLE BAY WITHIN LAKE MEAD NATIONAL RECREATION AREA (NRA). In low water years, the town of Callville appears above receding water lines and visitors can still visit the old town by hiking an easy one-mile trail from the resort. Otherwise, said scuba gear is in order. Find the Callville trail by heading east from Henderson on Lake Mead Parkway (SR 564) into Lake Mead NRA for 23 miles to a brown pointer sign to "Callville Bay." Follow this all the way into the resort where you'll find the well-signed trailhead and interpretive signs behind the gardens overlooking the lake.

Most Common Plant

Ah, our state flower. It's a plant only a Nevadan could love. Even the word "sagebrush" depicts images of boundless rolling expanses, rolling sunsets, or even the very notion of discovery.

It's certainly a plant to which nobody really glances. Its pungent odor, scraggly appearance, and monotone getup amidst often-bleak surroundings don't really help the poor thing either. In most eyes, the sagebrush might seem like a lazy choice for a state flower when compared to the Hibiscus, the Magnolia, or the Pacific Rhododendron. What the sagebrush lacks in beauty it makes up for in its tenacity and sheer resilience to survive.

Much like Nevada herself, wouldn't you say?

Big Role for Big Sagebrush

Also known as the Big Sage *(Artemisia tridentata)*, this hardy shrub displays an important role of identity and ecological significance here in the West, accounting for half of the state's vegetation. Yes, half, making it the MOST COMMON PLANT WE HAVE HERE IN THE SILVER STATE. Even though it is so abundant and so symbolic of where we live, it's remarkable how little people truly know about their state flower. Well, there's one person's account for the sagebrush:

> *"Sagebrush is a very fair fuel, but as a vegetable it is a distinguished failure. Nothing can abide the taste of it but the jackass and his illegitimate child the mule."*

Sam, you're half right there.

We've broken down a few compelling tidbits to prove Mr. Clemens wrong.

Here, There and Everywhere

The Big Sagebrush is the primary vegetation across vast and arid sections of the western United States and southwestern Canada. You can find it just about anywhere from 4,000 to 10,000 feet in elevation. From valleys to barren mountain slopes...even the far reaches of the tree line.

Wise in the Ways of Water

Perhaps even more remarkable is the way this plant harnesses every drop of precious moisture. The Big Sage uses lateral and deep spreading taproots to permeate deep soils and take advantage of all available seepage.

I'd Bottle That Up!

Sagey is most known for its robust fragrance that becomes full-bodied during wet or moist conditions, especially after thunderstorms! As pleasing as the odor is to us, it's thought to be one of the many survival tactics it employs to discourage browsing animals.

Great for Mind, Body, and Soul

Leaves from the Big Sage are toxic to both humans and most mammals, yet paradoxically, considered medicinally important by native peoples for thousands of years. Teas were regularly made from the leaves and used to cure a great variety of ailments from stomach aches to eye soreness. The boughs were burned for ceremonial rituals and air purification, while the bark was used to make rope, nets, and garments such as sandals and keep sacks.

Wise in Wind and Fire

Sagebrush is also highly susceptible to fire, relying on wind-blown seed dispersal for its growth. Any avid camper knows that stalks of sagebrush provide the perfect fuel and even a small branch will create a fire that burns long and hot. In fact, native people relied on it for thousands of winters thanks to its reliable burn potential and used as a common fuel for cooking and roasting pinyon nuts.

The importance of the sagebrush has sparked great interest and much-needed ecological awareness to a habitat that is all-too-often deemed worthless throughout the West. For example, the Greater Sage Grouse and Pygmy Rabbit are just two species that are fiercely dependent on it; they are born, live, breed, feed, and die within one shrub throughout its entire life. Efforts have arisen to conserve the many species that rely upon on this miracle plant for survival.

The Great Basin Sagebrush might not be the most beautiful state flower out there, but it'll certainly outlive the other 49.

Most Common Tree

In a landscape short on trees, author Stephen Trimble describes the Pinyon-Juniper woodland perfectly:

> *"One sturdy Pinion Pine or a family clustered together, are the only dependable woods in the Great Basin."*

The Singleleaf Pinyon Pine *(Pinus monophyla)* covers a dependable forty percent of the landscape in the Great Basin and roughly a third of all landscapes here in Nevada. Contrary to its harsh exterior, Nevada's tree variety is immense: from Quaking Aspen to pine, fir and even spruce forests.

Every forest and range begins with the Singleleaf Pinyon Pine, which indicates the transition zone of sagebrush valleys to mountain range. This important transition explains why the Pinyon Pine is the MOST ABUNDANT TREE IN NEVADA.

We're Pining for this Pine!

This sturdy and hardy evergreen dominates a biome that biologists call the *Pinyon-Juniper Woodland*: a landscape that typically occurs from about 5,000 feet in elevation to about 8,000 feet. This elevation is always consistent too, so precise in fact that Nevada regulars can easily judge their location throughout the state based on the presence of the Pinyon alone.

PJ Woodlands

These elvin forests can be impenetrable, yet lifesaving in the deep outback of Nevada as dependable cover, as well as a tremendous habitat for a variety of wildlife.

The Singleleaf Pinyon is unique among other pine trees in having a *fascicle* (needle bundle) of only one needle, hence its common and Latin names. Its short stature—typically ten to thirty feet tall and very slow-growing, requires thirty to sixty years to reach reproductive maturity.

Admit It. You'd go nuts too!

There's one "nutty" trait that sets this tree apart. The Pinyon has been a harbinger for life in the Great Basin for thousands of years as a dependable food source thanks to their meaty pine nuts, available for harvest in the fall.

A single tree can spread hundreds to thousands of pine nuts about every three to four years, depending on the age and location of the tree. Pine nut harvesting provided a staple food source and became closely linked with the cultures of native peoples of the Great Basin, many of whom continue traditional harvests today.

Nevadans young and old should feel privileged with the opportunity to partake in annual pine nut harvesting. Eat 'em raw or baked, salted or sugared.

The pinyon is just as much as a Nevadan as the rest of us. And we certainly would not be the same without this stout and sexy tree.

Steepest Grade

With Nevada's mountains come some wicked roads, both paved and gravel marvels. We've trodden our fair share.

The remote four-wheel-drive monster up to Mt. Washington in Great Basin National Park.

The roller coaster we call Kingsbury Grade.

The devilishly deceiving Hamilton Pass, or Black Grade near Jarbidge in Elko County.

None of them are as sinister as Geiger Grade connecting Reno and Silver City. Geiger Grade averages a nasty 21.4 percent gradient for much of its length, providing an unyielding tap of the brakes for over 30 miles!

Immediately upon leaving South Reno, State Route 341 begins an unrelenting climb up the Flowery Range in an attempt to conquer over 2,000 feet in just ten miles. Upon reaching Virginia City, the highway splits with SR 342 and continues another nasty downgrade of 19.4% for twelve more miles to Silver City and its eventual end with US 50.

These two consecutive pitches of grade garners a difference of 5,100 feet in elevation—an incredible feat considering the short 31-mile distance between Reno and Silver City.

At its most harrowing point, Greiner's Bend on SR 342 in Gold Hill circumvents a quarter-mile hairpin turn at a 29% grade. This bend is especially nasty because of its tight two additional switchbacks that occur on an already sloping curve! Every winter, this grade is responsible for stalling out even the most well-equipped vehicles.

So why the twisty pavement? The Nevada Department of Transportation simply paved over the original wagon route; to this day, Geiger Grade is the most direct route to and from the Comstock.

Rarest Fish in the World

The Amargosa Desert is located just over the Funeral Mountains of Death Valley National Park, an area notorious as the hottest and driest location in the Western Hemisphere. So then, conceive the possibility that directly below the surface lies an ancient pool that may connect to other parts of the world.

Enter Devil's Hole— a mystery pit that has been preserved since 1984 solely for the protection of the world's rarest fish: the Devil's Hole pupfish found nowhere else on the planet.

After all, this is the Nevada where nothing is ever as it seems.

The Mystery Unfolds

Scientists estimate the Devils Hole Pupfish *(Cyprinodon diabolis)* has lived under the desert in isolation for upwards of 25,000 years. The hole was formed about 60,000 years ago in an event where the earth suddenly burst open.

Around 12,000 years ago, the hole became isolated and the cavern filled with fossil water, or paleowater over a span of 15,000 years!

The water within Devil's Hole is crystal clear, holds a constant temperature of 92°F, and is the only suitable environment for the tiny Pupfish that forage and spawn exclusively on a shallow rock shelf only a few feet wide. The hole itself measures only 8 feet by 60 feet in diameter— beckoning us to probe what lies beneath this tiny opening in the earth.

At a glance of the surrounding barren desert, it's hard to fathom that beneath the surface lies a system of sprawling water-filled caves.

The exact depth of Devil's Hole is the stuff of nightmares as it has yet to be reached or recorded! Dozens of people have died trying to find the base of this seemingly bottomless pit. Some scientists believe the hole could be as deep as a quarter mile, but more eerily, we can ask: where does it go?

Researchers also speculate that it could be connected to other parts of the world. Earthquakes as far as Indonesia have caused the waters of Devil's Hole to splash and slosh like water in a bathtub. In 2012, a 7.2 magnitude earthquake in Mexico (some 2,000 miles away) created waves over six feet above normal levels!

These seismic waves have been likened to mini underground tsunamis and to this day continue to occur when the earth shakes halfway around the globe. Devil's Hole is a window into the earth's hydrologic past, and a portal into a seemingly endless world.

> 📍 DEVIL'S HOLE IS A 40-ACRE DETACHED UNIT OF DEATH VALLEY NATIONAL PARK LOCATED WITHIN THE ASH MEADOWS NATIONAL WILDLIFE REFUGE, 29 MILES WEST OF PAHRUMP. To see it for yourself, follow Bell Vista Road west out of Pahrump for about 40 minutes to the Wildlife Refuge. Here, you'll find brown NPS pointer signs to Devil's Hole. The entrance to the hole is fenced off with an electric barrier to first and foremost protect the endangered pupfish, but also to prevent certain bipedal idiots from drowning in its waters. You can view the hole via an official overlook into the hole.

The Most Remote Town with Services

For decades the tiny mountain hamlet of Jarbidge has been given the cool title of "Nevada's Most Remote Town." It's a sacred title that Nevadans hold dear. Even state brochures and travel guides are quick to adorn it as "most remote," "most isolated" and so forth. For those of us who have been to Jarbidge, yes, we will attest at how damn remote it really is. There's no denying that its off-the-grid location and cool setting as the last stagecoach robbery of the west in 1918 has the goods for a great story.

Here's what a Google search pulled up when we typed "Jarbidge, Most Remote Town":

"Located 10 miles south of the Idaho-Nevada border is the small community of Jarbidge. Home to just a handful of people, it's considered the most remote town in the entire state. You won't find any paved roads within a 20-mile radius of Jarbidge."

But there is a keyword here: *considered*.

Researching the Remote Factor

Jarbidge is far from being the state's *most* remote town. Yeah, it can only be reached from Nevada by a single graded road, and in winter only from Idaho...but is this really the only reason?

While defining "remote" is a subjective term here in Nevada, we used a strict parameter and three qualifications in which to base our decision here. We've omitted rural ranches, mining operations, and outposts, such as Tonkin, Rawhide, and Middlegate respectively.

Instead, we counted only communities with a zip code, bonafide services *and* a year-round population. It needed to meet all three. Geography is tricky, but it never lies. This wasn't a superlative drawn easy and we're prepared for a lot of surprise from other well-versed Nevadans.

After triple-checking the maps and a boatload of buildup, we discovered that the mini burg of MCDERMITT IS FURTHER AWAY FROM ANY NEIGHBORING POPULATION CENTER IN NEVADA.

Nestled on the Oregon-Nevada state line, this tiny border community is 70 miles north of Paradise Valley, the closest nearest community in any direction! By heading north on US 95, you'll encounter the next (and only) major services 101 miles away in Jordan Valley, Oregon. By driving west on SR 140, you won't find anything else until Denio Junction for 108 miles! You will find one gas station 51 miles to the south, but it is not considered a permanent place of habitation, but an outpost like the ones stated earlier.

We meticulously mapped every remote town in the state that we could find and McDermitt always came up with the furthest distance.

In comparison, the nearest community to Jarbidge is Rogerson, Idaho: a commendable 64 miles away, but a little shy of McDermitt's impressive distance from Paradise Valley. Sorry, Jarbidge. You're just not that remote after all.

So the next time you read an article toting Jarbidge as the state's "most remote town," giggle freely as you whisper the real answer to yourself... And maybe call up the state tourism board to clear up the faux pas?

Hey now. Just a McMinute!

Not only is McDermitt the most remote town in Nevada, but it's a pretty interesting one that is uniquely Battle Born. This is one of only three Nevada communities that crosses state borders. The indiscriminate state line runs right through town, providing a bite-size headache for the states of Oregon and Nevada.

Around the turn of the century, the historic White Horse Inn, the town's claim to fame, provided the only means of services in this very desolate region of the Great Basin. Like a craft of genius, the inn was built right on the state line for a few reasons. If you visited the two-story inn, you could have a drink at the bar, game away, and partake in the *nightlife* on the Nevada side before having a no-sales-tax meal and lodging in the next room in Oregon.

Today, all businesses, including the Sinclair gas station, library, school, Say When Casino, and the town's only motel and restaurant, sit about 500-1000 feet inside of Nevada. Petitions were made in the 1980's to relocate all businesses (except the casino) to the Oregon side to take advantage of Oregon's no-sales-tax.

However, look closely and you'll see the town's only post office is on the *Oregon side* of the border.

The presence of a post office dictates an entire town's physical and legitimate existence. So, by these parameters, technically McDermitt, *Nevada* doesn't exist. So, do we call it McDermitt, Oregon?

Thanks, McDermitt. We've got a massive headache now.

Most Remote Towns in Nevada

Why not spend the day and scurry to these remote locales across the state? Fuel up the entire tank because that's about how much you'll need to get to these fascinating forays.

1. **McDermitt** - Nearest services: Paradise Valley (70 miles) – Next: Jordan Valley, OR. (101 miles)

2. **Jarbidge** - Nearest services: Rogerson, ID. (64 miles) – Next: Mountain City (78 miles)

3. **Baker** - Nearest services: Ely (62 miles) – Next: Delta, UT. (96 miles)

4. **Austin** - Nearest services: Carvers (59 miles) – Next: Eureka (70 miles)

5. **Gerlach** - Nearest services: Nixon (59 miles) - Next: Wadsworth (75 miles)

6. **Gabbs** - Nearest services Hawthorne (56 miles) – Next: Fallon (79 miles)

7. **Rachel** - Nearest services: Alamo (52 miles) – Next: Tonopah (109 miles)

8. **Tuscarora** - Nearest services: Elko (52 miles) - Next: Owyhee (61 miles)

9. **Jackpot** - Nearest services: Twin Falls, ID. (47 miles) – Next: Wells (68 miles)

10. **Belmont** - Nearest services: Tonopah (46 miles) – Next: Austin (96 miles)

A Couple More Teasers

Ready for some more?

Having been to every corner of the Silver State in search of these awesome superlatives we hope you're as exhausted and satisfied as we are!

Now that you've had your fill of this juicy meal, it's time to cool down with a few final refreshers. Every savory buffet needs a chocolate mousse, and before we bring you the grand finale, we wanted to honor the few places in Nevada that didn't quite make the book for a number of reasons...

...Time constraints, page substance, lack of supporting viable material, or things that fell just shy of earning superlative status. A few were even because of my screaming feral children. Not Kidding.

Yup. These are Runners Up. Baby Sidekicks. Honorable Mentions...but absolutely winners in our eyes.

Virgin Valley Fire Opal

The Virgin Valley of northern Humboldt County is the only known site in the world where opal forms inside of wood casts, a process in nature so rare that it occurs in only three-known spots in the state. The most notable specimen of the prized rock sits in the Smithsonian behind tempered glass with an eye-watering value of $100,000.

Nevada's Only "Indian War"

May 20, 1868 marks the Battle of Pyramid Lake, the only documented "war" in Nevada history. This deadly battle lasted for a month as retaliation against brutalities committed by white settlers from Virginia City.

Largest Church

Standing 179 feet tall in Gothic-style exuberance is St. Mary's in the Mountains Catholic Church in Virginia City. Ironically, this beauty remains one of the few structures that survived the Great Fire of 1875. Divine intervention perhaps?

Highest Community

The pine forested hamlet of Mt. Charleston Village in Clark County sits at 7,510 feet above sea level. "The Village" came into existence around 1960 with the construction of the Mt. Charleston Ski Resort. Of course, the community's 350 year-round residents eagerly await a bustling tourist base from November through April during ski season.

SILVER STATE SUPERLATIVES

Largest County (in size)

Nye County in Central Nevada covers 18,159 square miles—the fourth largest county in the lower 48, and a county so vast, it takes up real estate in all three regions of the state. This is a county so large it could easily contain the states of New Jersey, Delaware, New Hampshire, Vermont, Rhode Island, and Connecticut combined.

Largest County (in population)

While Nye holds the title for size, Clark County is Nevada's most populous county with a staggering 2.3 million people. Clark County alone makes up approximately 73% of the entire state's population.

"The Crookedest Railroad in the West"

While not a true superlative, this was the nickname given to the Virginia & Truckee Railroad because of its numerous hairpin curves, two trestles, and notoriously steep pitches throughout its short 14-mile length.

Largest Spherical Object in the World

New to the game in 2023, the MSG Sphere at the Venetian in Las Vegas is the largest round ... well, *thing* in the world. The massive ball stands at 365 feet tall and 516 feet across, encompassing 580,000 LED lights that dazzle spectators for streaming premium live shows and broadcasts.

Longest Hiking Trail

This prestigious title belongs to the airy 72-mile Toiyabe Crest Trail (TCT) of the Arc Dome Wilderness in Central Nevada. This beloved wilderness destination rides the spine of the Toiyabe Range at an average elevation of 9,200 feet, coincidentally, one of the longest roadless areas in the state.

World Land Speed Record

In 2002, American Sam Whittington set the world record of 81 mph for a solo rider on a bicycle on State Route 305 south of Battle Mountain. In 1983, an Englishman on the Black Rock Desert contributed another equally famous speed record, bragging a whopping 633.468 mph—enough to break the sound barrier and leave a tough record for anyone else to best.

Three Nevada Towns Located One Hour in the Future

The small border communities of Owyhee, Jackpot, and West Wendover are the only towns in Nevada set one hour ahead of the rest of the state. The Mountain Time Zone was extended to include these three little communities so residents could better conduct business with the neighboring states of Idaho and Utah.

Highest Mining Camp

The ghost girl of Treasure City in White Pine County was perched at an elevation of 9,153 feet—the highest established camp in Nevada history. The camp's life was brief after a discovery of silver ore in 1869. Residents quickly moved onto lower (and more comfortable!) prospecting in lower elevations less than a year later.

Oldest Cattle Ranch

The 1,700-acre Cushman-Corkill Ranch in Fallon has been in continuous operation since 1861. At the completion of the Newlands Reclamation Project in 1903, the Cushman family began raising alfalfa, corn, potatoes, Sudan grass, and small grains for the future.

First Female Sheriff

In March 1919, voters elected Clara Crowell, Nevada's first female sheriff. Crowell's win over several male applicants turned many heads. Amazingly, her victory came just two weeks before the 19th Amendment, giving American women the right to vote. One of her most memorable moments as Sheriff came when she posed as a Native American woman to catch a man illegally selling liquor to Native Americans. In the act she flung open her coat revealing her badge.

Highest Lake Accessible by Road

Angel Lake sits at a cozy 8,378' above sea level at the end of SR 231. Angel is completely enclosed by dramatic glacial cirques within a deep granite bowl, a result of the same intense glaciation as the neighboring Ruby Mountains. For Angel, it's almost miraculous that such a stunning scene sits just twenty minutes above the dry desert floor.

Smallest TV Station

Next time you're in Hawthorne, tune into *TV13 (or KWI)* for Bob and Virginia Becker's network. TV13 is an FCC-licensed television station that broadcasts a multitude of mostly older shows, while also including breaking news stories about the region that come around every once in a blue moon.

Largest Lake Entirely Within Nevada

Possibly the most beautiful desert lake in America, Pyramid Lake is the largest body of water completely within state lines: a cobalt blue sea some 9 miles wide, 27 miles long, and 168 feet at its deepest point. This ancient sea has become a stronghold and world-class fishery for the endemic and endangered Lahontan Cutthroat Trout.

First (Oldest) Wilderness Area in Nevada

Established in 1964, the 113,000-acre Jarbidge Wilderness was the forethought of Nevada's first initiative to preserve its remarkable landscape. Within the Jarbidge Wilderness is an exotic wildland of dripping fir forests, icy lakes, and varying peaks and sawtooth ridges to 10,000 feet.

World's Largest Eatery

The next time you have a craving for, well, everything, visit the Carnival World Buffet inside the Rio in Las Vegas. This iconic feast is the world's largest dining experience with more than 200 selections of ethnic variety and 70 types of homemade desserts.

Largest concentration of fossils

The epoch represented at Tule Springs Fossil Beds National Monument brings education and exploration of many Ice Age creatures, including the Columbian Mammoth, extinct horses, camels and bison, and the dire wolf. It is the largest concentration of fossils in the Silver State.

Best Preserved Mining Camp

The mining camp of Berlin in central Nevada never prospered to the same extent as other boom towns in state history, and its low population accounts for the town's excellent state of preservation today. The town sits fully preserved in a state of arrested decay within Berlin-Ichthyosaur State Park, a whopping 1.5 hours east of Fallon.

Oldest Reservation

Formed in 1859 and legally reserved in 1874, the Pyramid Lake Reservation is the oldest Native American reservation in the United States. It's also the America's second-largest reservation at 476,728 acres, smaller only to the Navajo Nation of the Four Corners.

Largest Gold Mine in North America

Since its opening, the Goldstrike Mine north of Carlin, employs over 2,000 Nevadans and has squeezed out some 42 million ounces of gold in its lifetime. As of this writing, the largest gold mine on the continent plunges 3,700 feet into the earth and has been in continuous operation 24/7/365 since 1986.

Stateline Pool

It is here at the Cal-Neva Resort in Crystal Bay that Frank Sinatra was banned from all casinos in Nevada, but perhaps more famous is its state line swimming pool frequented by Marilyn Monroe that spans the California-Nevada border. That's right. Be the cool kid and swim in both states at once! Got Marilyn? The resort is also supposedly haunted by the very active ghosts of these two celebrities.

Tallest Building

The 67-story Fontainebleau hotel-casino on the Las Vegas Strip is the tallest fully habitable building in Nevada, with a height of 642 feet and costing a starry $300 per night. The Fontainebleau was a long-awaited addition after sitting empty for ten years.

Largest Animal

With an average weight of 400 pounds, the American Black Bear *(Ursus americanus)* is the state's largest animal and the only naturally occurring bear species in Nevada. Most of our bears are concentrated in the Carson Range, but a few scattered populations have been found in small populations across the state.

Only Singing Dunes in the World

Along with the Kelso Dunes in California, the Crescent Dunes, Sand Mountain and Big Dune are the only supposed "singing dunes" in the world. The dunes emit a buzzing-to-high-pitched screech in very rare instances caused by the right combination of timing, shifting sands, and the humidity of the air.

The Most Isolated Spot in Nevada

So, we're going to begin by giving ourselves credit where credit is due. Finding the factual numbers on this one was an absolute battle and surmounted for more research than any other superlative in this manifesto.

First, we have to throw in the obligatory safety disclaimer here. Oh yeah, we're busting out the italics for this one.

Although the following GPS and directions are factual, things such as weather, personal preparations, and world circumstances will elicit some factors beyond our control. If you choose to follow this plot, please take charge of your own decisions and preparation requirements.

Now that we have that out of the way, strap in and hold on tight. We're ending this shindig with a bang.

If you've ever wanted to know the best place to go to escape people and be guaranteed solitude, we've found it.

Reaching Isolation

It's fair to say that the word "remote" is subjective here in Nevada, but once again, we used a strict parameter in which to base our decision. The following GPS coordinates plot the absolute farthest spot in relation to *any major population center*. Like McDermitt, we are not counting rural ranches, mining operations, or outposts. So, believe us. There's plenty of openness to go around!

For this coveted twilight zone, we're stepping far into the Northwest corner of Nevada, over 200 miles from Reno.

> From this location, let's roll the stats, boys and girls:
> Gerlach: *71.1 miles*
> Denio: *89.2 miles*
> Cedarville, CA: *89.9 miles*
> Winnemucca: *123 miles*
> McDermitt: *134 miles*
> Imlay: *157 miles*
> Adel, OR: *168 miles*

The coordinates, **41.362687, -119.025528** plops you just inside the southern boundary of the North Black Rock Range Wilderness. The nearest form of habitation is the Soldier Meadows Guest Ranch, but reaching the roadside requires a drive of 28.2 miles and an agonizing 45 minutes just from the ranch. Tack another half-day drive from the nearest community, in this case Gerlach, and well ... this might as well be a multi-day sojourn.

Even though the ranch is just six air miles as the Mountain Bluebird flies, any form of help will seem like worlds away. Getting to the actual coordinates can only be done by scrambling north up a tangled ridge from an already rough four-wheel-drive road.

This tire-popping path is known as Paiute Creek Road and directly connects with SR 140 (near Leonard Creek) in about two hours-time. This road also defines the southern boundary of the North Black Rock Range Wilderness—a wild land *known* for its isolation factor.

The best point of reference here is Slumgullion Creek which snakes its way through the range in a shallow canyon. We've tried plotting to this set of coordinates many times with Google Maps, and Google Earth reveals a mere tiny depression at best with no real frame of reference.

We've decided to lay it out for you ourselves, proudly and painstakingly.

Getting Gone to the Most Remote Spot

We're basing our directions from Gerlach, the nearest community with services. Find Gerlach by heading east from Reno-Sparks on Interstate 80 for 32 miles to Wadsworth (Exit 43). Turn left onto SR 447 and proceed another 75 miles.

In Gerlach, head north from Bruno's Country Club to County Route 34 continuing for twelve miles to Soldier Meadows Road (Humboldt County Route 208). Here is when you leave the pavement for 64.3 long miles.

In about three hours you'll arrive at "Paiute Creek Road" (named by the owners of the Paiute Creek Ranch).

After crossing a cattle guard at around mile 64, look for this road as it heads east into a high set of mountains. Although this road is mostly navigable by BLM standards, *do not attempt to drive this route in wet weather!*

It's here you'll leave the safety of the well-graded gravel of the Soldier Meadows Road (CR 208) and turn right. This road juts across the valley and deteriorates suddenly. Tighten the belt. Now the adventure begins.

Follow this route for 4.3 horrible miles. Here, the road will split and the widest and most traversed path swings southward. You'll know you're on the right road when you cross Slumgullion Creek in one mile. Crossing the creek can be a mere four inches deep to a raging torrent of a foot or more in wetter months, so take extra caution here!

In another three miles, this road wraps around the Wilderness Boundary in a long 180° swing.

This is your first indication that you're close.

The actual coordinates at **41.362687, -119.025528** cannot be reached by road. *It's imperative that you research your best BLM maps specifically for Black Rock Desert or Humboldt County regions.* Then, and only then, make your best decision.

When you're close, park along the road and begin walking up the ridge. Even if you're off by a few degrees, this is THE MOST REMOTE PLACE YOU CAN GET IN NEVADA with the possibility of not seeing another person for days. There are a few geocaches near this spot to help you out. People come into the Northwest Corner for one reason: to get gone. This is the real Nevada without the fixings and the press.

Seeking Solitude Elsewhere

In case you weren't satisfied with the set of coordinates we presented you, here are some of other very remote areas in Nevada you can escape to without ever seeing another person. Some of these are easier to reach than others, but all of them will require a determination and fearless face to branch away from the beaten path. Risk and reward.

Though these may not fit our criteria of "most remote" for this book, these could very well be winners in your eyes.

Owyhee Desert

This bleak wasteland covers sixty square miles along the Oregon border centered on the South Fork Owyhee River in Elko County. The dominating presence of salt scrub and iodine bush means this is a true barren desert. According to the US Geological Survey (USGS), it's estimated the entirety of the Owyhee Desert is home to less than 200 people.

Nevada-Idaho-Oregon Tri-Corner Monument

This lonely monument is one of the most isolated border corners in the country accessible only by a rough 50-mile one-way in-and-out jeep track from McDermitt. Any points surrounding the monument, northwest into Oregon, northeast into Idaho, or south into Nevada, will be mostly inaccessible.

Goose Creek Basin

This isolated northeast corner of the state sees less than ten cars per week and an average of 35 people per day (mostly ranchers). Roads are impassable for half the year from all directions. The best way to access this area is by the California Emigrant Trail National Backcountry Byway. Look for the signed turnoff in between Jackpot and Contact in northeastern Elko County. From here, it is roughly 45 miles into this region.

Lunar Crater and Rainbow Valley

Accessed by the Lunar Crater National Backcountry Byway, Rainbow Valley is an underrated gem of wild lands and incredible geologic wonders. Its isolated location right in the middle of "the ghost stretch" on US 6 (in between Ely and Tonopah) means you will find very few people out here, but plenty of sweet Nevada bliss!

Worthington Mountains Wilderness

Anybody who finds themselves in this wilderness area did so on purpose. The Worthington Mountains are nowhere near anything, but those willing to brave rarely driven four-wheel-drive roads will find features that few Nevadans will ever see. In fact, the Worthington ranks among the top five most isolated wilderness areas in the country with a visitation of less than 400 people per year. Try on its massive 300-foot tall cave on for size.

Enjoyed this work? Don't forget to review Silver State Superlatives! The best way to support an indie author is to review their work, so <u>please scan below and visit my linktree</u>to easily find me and my works. While you're there, throw me a good pun and tell me your thoughts!

Scan Me

Resources

ATLAS OBSCURA. *THE REPUBLIC of Molossia*, 2020.

Benchmark Maps, *Nevada Road & Recreation Atlas*, Sixth Edition. Benchmark Maps, 2022.

Benson L., Hattori E., Southon J., Aleck B., 2013. *Dating North America's Oldest Petroglyphs, Winnemucca Lake sub-basin, Nevada*. Journal of Archaeological Science, Vol. 40, No. 12, pp. 4466-4476; doi: 10.1016/j.jas.2013.06.022

Black Rock Desert-High Rock Canyon Emigrant Trails National Conservation Area, https://www.blm.gov/visit/black-rock-desert-high-rock-canyon-emigrant-trails-national-conservation-area

Bowers, Michael W. *The Sagebrush State: Nevada's History, Government, and Politics*, Fifth Edition. University of Nevada Press, 2018.

Caesars Rewards. *Restaurant Guy Savoy,* https://www.caesars.com/caesars-palace/restaurants/guy-savoy

Carlson, Helen S. *Nevada Place Names: A Geographical Dictionary*, University of Nevada Press, 1996.

Casino Life Magazine, *Biggest Slot Machine Wins in History*, 2018.

Chung, Su Kim. *Las Vegas Then and Now*, Pavilion Press, 2016.

Clark, Jeanna L. *Nevada Wildlife Viewing Guide*, Falcon Press, 1993.

Cummins, Joseph, Inglis, James, Stone, Barry. *The Almost Complete History of the World*, Metro Books, 2012.

"Dayton vs Genoa." *Wild Nevada*. Season 6, Episode 6, PBS Reno, 2023.

Denton, Craig. *People of the West Desert: Finding Common Ground*, Utah State University Press, 1999.

DeSilva, Kristen. *5 Places in Nevada You Can Be in 3 States at Once*, Las Vegas Review-Journal, 2016.

Duggan, Brian, "Tracking down Nevada History," *Nevada Appeal*, January 18, 2011.

Friends of Nevada Wilderness. *Referenced: Arc Dome Wilderness, East Humboldt Wilderness, Jarbidge Wilderness, North Schell Wilderness, North Black Rock Range Wilderness, Ruby Mountains Wilderness, Worthington Mountains Wilderness*, Reno Office, Reno, NV. 2020.

Genoa Bar and Saloon. *Genoa Bar and Saloon: About the Bar.*

Great Big Story. *This Man Runs a Micronation of 32 People*, CNN's Great Big Story, 2016.

Gibson, Daniel and Roosevelt, Theodore IV. *Audubon Guide to the National Wildlife Refuges: Southwest, Arizona, Nevada, New Mexico, Texas*, St. Martin's Griffin, 2000.

Grubbs, Bruce. *Exploring Great Basin National Park including Mount Moriah Wilderness*, Bright Angel Press, 2012.

Hall, Shawn. *Romancing Nevada's Past: Ghost Towns And Historic Sites Of Eureka, Lander, And White Pine Counties*, University of Nevada Press; 1st edition, 2016.

Hart, John. *Hiking the Great Basin, The High Desert Country of California, Nevada, Oregon, and Utah*, Sierra Club Books, 1991.

Hitchcock, Don. *Winnemucca Lake Petroglyphs: Oldest Rock Art in North America*, 2018.

Hopkins, Sarah Winnemucca. *Life Among the Piutes, Their Wrongs and Claims*, Classic Reprint, Forgotten Books, 2018.

Hulse, James W. *The Silver State: Nevada's Heritage Reinterpreted*, Third Edition, University of Nevada Press, 2004.

Guinness World Records. *Land Speed (Fastest Car)*. 1997.

Inyo National Forest. Referenced: *Boundary Peak Trailhead, White Mountain Peak*, 2024.

James, Ronald M. and Susan A. *A Short History of Virginia City*, University of Nevada Press, 2014.

Las Vegas Convention and Visitors Authority. *Referenced: "Visit Las Vegas," Empathy Suite"*, Las Vegas, NV. 2020.

"Lost in the Snow." *I Shouldn't Be Alive*. Season 1, Episode 2, Darlow Smithson Productions, 2005.

Masn Nationals. "Hubert Keller Gives Cooking Demonstration of $5000 Burger." *YouTube* video, 6:39. December 11, 2018. https://youtu.be/tLZQeuSXYzk

Mitchell, Roger & Loris. *Great Basin SUV Trails: Volume II, Southwestern Nevada – A Backcountry Guide to 34 Four-Wheeling Adventures in Southwestern Nevada*, Track & Trail Publications, 2005.

Moreno, Richard. *Roadside History of Nevada*, Mountain Press, 2000.

National Park Service, Referenced: *Great Basin National Park, Lake Mead National Recreation Area, Tule Springs National Monument*, United States Department of the Interior, 2020.

Nevada Department of Transportation. *Referenced: 2020, 2021, 2022, 2023, 2024 Description Index of State Highways and Interstates*, Carson City, NV. 2024.

Nevada Gaming Control Board. *Email to confirm the oldest gaming license in Nevada, Attn: Department of Gaming Research.* 2024.

Nevada Mining. *The Mineral That Started a Modern-Day Boom.* 2022.

Nevada State Parks. *Referenced: Berlin-Ichthyosaur, Elgin Schoolhouse, Ice Age Fossils, Lake Tahoe-Nevada, Mormon Station, Old Las Vegas Mormon Fort, Valley of Fire*, Carson City, NV. 2020.

Online Nevada Encyclopedia (ONE). Articles Referenced: *Burning Man, Comstock Mining District, Delamar, Elgin, Eureka, Genoa, Great Basin Bristlecone Pine, Humboldt River, Ice Age Nevada and Lake Lahontan, Las Vegas, Old Mormon Fort, Reese River Valley, Rock Art of Nevada, Sand Mountain, Salt Desert Vegetation of Nevada, Sarah Winnemucca, Singing Dunes, Spirit Cave Man: The Controversy, Singleleaf Pinyon, Valley of Fire, Virginia City and Gold Hill* 2013-2023.

Paher, Stanley. *Nevada Ghost Towns & Mining Atlas*, Nevada Publications, 2006.

Pizarro, Kris Ann, Ross, Christian, and Tingley, Joseph V. *Geologic and Natural History Tours in the Reno Area: Expanded Edition (Special Publication 19)*, Nevada Bureau of Mines and Geology, 2005.

Pizarro, Kriss Ann and Tingley, Joseph V. *Traveling America's Loneliest Road: A Geologic and Natural History Tour through Nevada along US Highway 50*, Nevada Bureau of Mines and Geology, 2000.

Plant Maps. *Nevada Record High and Low Temperatures Map*. 2020.

Restaurant Guy Savoy. *Restaurant Guy Savoy,* https://guysavoy.com/eu

Schullery, Paul. *America's National Parks: The Spectacular Forces That Shaped Our Treasured Lands*, DK Publishing, 2002.

Sebesta, Stanley Paul. "Carson City Man Visits Every Single Nevada Landmark." *YouTube* video, 2:03. February 1, 2011.

Statista. *Number of slot machines and other mobile gaming devices in casinos in Nevada from 1965 to 2018*. https://www.statista.com/statistics/250168/slot-machines-in-nevada/#:~:text=In%20the%20U.S.%20state%20of,devices%20in%20casinos%20in%202018.

St. John, Alan D. *Oregon's Dry Side: Exploring East of the Cascade Crest*, Timber Press Inc., 2007.

Stebbins, Samuel. "*What's the Richest Town in Every State?*", 24/7 Wall Street, USA Today. May 30, 2018.

Sumner, Bob. *Hiking Nevada's County High Points*, Spotted Dog Press, Inc. 2010.

Tahoe Fund. *Tahoe's Fun Facts*, Tahoe City, CA. 2020.

Timko, Steve. *20 years ago, rescue saved family after 8 days stuck in snow*. Reno-Gazette Journal, 2013.

Tisinger, Danielle. *Textual Performance and the Western Frontier: Sarah Winnemucca Hopkins's" Life Among the Piutes: Their Wrongs and Claims"."* Western American Literature (2002).

Toll, David W. *The Complete Nevada Traveler*, Gold Hill Publishing Co., 2002.

Travel Nevada, Referenced: "*State of Nevada*," Carson City, NV. 2020.

Trimble, Stephen. *The Sagebrush Ocean, Special Edition*, University of Nevada Press, 1999.

The Strat: Hotel, Casino & Skypod. Referenced: *Attractions*, Las Vegas, NV. 2020.

White, Mike. *Afoot & Afield: Tahoe-Reno – 201 Spectacular Outings in the Lake Tahoe Region*, Wilderness Press, 2016.

White, Michael C. *Nevada Wilderness Areas and Great Basin National Park: A Hiking and Backpacking Guide*, Wilderness Press, 1997.

Acknowledgments

This book wouldn't be possible without the many friendly faces I have met throughout my nine-year journey across Nevada, cool peeps who have volunteered their time, ideas, suggestions, and resonating passion for their state. I know I would leave out a few of these devoted and wonderful souls, so I won't even try to name them individually. Instead, I'll just say a fervent *thank you* to everyone I met along the way.

You know who you are.

Thank you to my lovely little girls, whom in about a decade will read this and call Daddy a complete dork for concocting such a meticulous rap sheet of nerdy information.

And to my beautiful wife, who knows I obsess over crafting the perfect manuscript. The end-result you hold in your hands wouldn't be possible without her proofreading, nit-pick editing, grammar patrol, and relentless eye for tyepos and mistaks.

Well, damn. I guess she missed a few.

About the Author

FROM 2004 TO 2013, Paul spent nine years driving the entire state of Nevada and became the first person to personally visit and catalog all 274 Nevada Historical Markers. His passion for storytelling has also brought him an opportunity to raise thousands of dollars for local Nevada non-profit organizations such as Friends of Nevada Wilderness through his public speaking and slideshow photography.

Today, Paul Sebesta is a French translator and interpreter, outdoor guide, freelance writer, and photographer extraordinaire, leading photography workshops and local tours in his backyard of Central Oregon. Just follow the scent of beef jerky and Mountain Dew.

When he isn't creating and curating projects, he sings (horribly off-key) or plays piano (wonderfully on-key) to his girls.

You can view his 9 year journey around the state of Nevada at **www.nv-landmarks.com.**

www.ingramcontent.com/pod-product-compliance
Lightning Source LLC
Chambersburg PA
CBHW052030030426
42337CB00027B/4944